Diary
of a
Camping Diva

*A practical, but fun guide for
surviving the great outdoors*

by
Dina Wills

Cover design by Jeff Byrd

This book is dedicated to
all the Divas out there.

(You know who you are.)

Special thanks go to

…My husband, Michael: If not for you, I wouldn't have had the time, experience or freedom to write this book in the first place, so thank you.

…My editor, Marlo; also Julie, Debbie, Mom, and Aunt Pat: Thanks ladies. I could *not* have finished this book without your guidance, love, and support.

Author Notes

As the saying goes...

Until I wrote this book, I didn't realize how often I use everyday expressions in my speech and writing. In fact, I open with one: "When I first started camping, *I couldn't see the forest for the trees.*" Which begs the question (see, I did it again); who was the first person to string these words together? So, I've decided to identify and explain each of them on my website (diaryofacampingdiva. com). Oh, and, by the way. I did mean to say "for the trees" and not "through the trees."

Gear Recommendations

As of March 10, 2015, the prices quoted in this book are current; however, please don't hold me accountable, as they will fluctuate. That said, in an effort to keep up with new gear, etc.; I'll be blogging about *everything* camping on my website.

"He" References

In order to keep things simple, whenever I mentioned an animal in this book (with the exception of female bears), I defaulted to a "he" reference. I hope this doesn't offend anyone.

You might be a Diva IF:

1. You ask the camp host where to find the breakfast buffet.

2. You think the ranger is there to set up your tent.

3. You're shocked and appalled that your tent doesn't have an outlet for your blow dryer.

4. You pack your Keurig.

5. You tell your camp neighbors that "quiet time" is until noon.

6. You look for the campfire switch.

7. You hike in heels.

8. You storm off with righteous indignation upon discovering the amphitheater doesn't show movies.

9. You scream, "Shut up!" at the crickets.

10. You complain that the moon is too bright.

CONTENTS

BACK MATTER

Preface

You Tarzan,
Me Not Necessarily Jane

May 25, 1996
<u>**Sedona, AZ (between a rock and a hard place)**</u>
  Note to self: I love not camping.

Bears smell. A lot. Once, a hungry 200 pounder crawled into our truck, and it took a full year to get rid of the stench he left behind. You're probably wondering what he smelled like. Well, this particular bear smelled like B.O., dirt, and poop. The fact that I know this boggles my mind because, prior to this encounter, the closest I'd come to a bear was at Disney's *Country Bear Jamboree*. But there it is.

How I came to share the same space with this opportunistic beast is a very long story, so I'll just give you the *Cliff Notes* version. I was motivated by love. Like Tarzan, my husband is a strong, silent, outdoorsman type, and prior to getting to know him, my idea of roughing it meant staying in a 3-Star, versus 4-Star resort. But he took my hand and showed me the way. Albeit, it wasn't necessarily the way I would have gone.

Our first romp into the woods together was, well, let's just say...rustic. We ended up pitching a tent in the middle of nowhere. Yes, nowhere does exist. There was no picnic table, no fire ring, no running water, and certainly no restroom. We just pulled off the side of the road and set up "camp" somewhere. That night I peed behind a bush, chewed a piece of gum in lieu of toothpaste, slept on the hard ground in my clothes, and woke up to something sniffing our tent. It was not fun.

My point? I'm telling you this, so it doesn't happen to you. I was naïve, but you don't have to be. My pain is your gain. So when your man starts pounding his chest and insists on exposing you to the elements, ask the following two questions:

1. What's the name of the campground?
2. Do we have a reservation?

If he doesn't have a plan, and he just wants to "wing it," trust me Diva, this trip isn't for you. Tell him to have fun and to give your regards to Mother Nature. But if he persists, then you're going to need some tips—and I have plenty of those, so read on, my friend. By the time you turn the last page of this book, you'll be an informed camper before your feet even hit the dirt. (Minus the regrettable campsite choices, mosquito bites, canned Spam, bear encounters, and bad hair.)

One

Camping 101:
Various Types, Explained

May 26, 2000
Mammoth Lakes, CA

Oh. My. God. Today I discovered the tent trailer. Strange that these two words, when separated, are so unappealing, but when strung together—oh so right!

When I first started camping, I couldn't see the forest for the trees. My husband, then boyfriend, would say something like this: "Hey, do you wanna go camping this weekend?" And I'd think, "God, no!" but I'd respond, "Sure, okay."

Back then, I didn't understand that I had options. The act itself was so foreign, it never occurred to me to question the specifics. But, after spending one too many nights sleeping in a flimsy little *no-insulation-whatsoever-to-buffer-the-cold* tent, I had an epiphany. I needed to stop the madness and negotiate a compromise. Soon after, I started looking around and realized that there are different types of camping and various ways to make each type bearable. So, without further ado, here are said options from most painful to least.

BACKPACKING

It's not rocket science, but for those of you who've never done it, let me spell it out for you. When you go backpacking, *you have to carry your stuff in a pack…on your back.* To be brutally honest, you couldn't pay me enough money to engage in this activity, but if *you* must, I suggest you go PPO'd.

- **P**repared.
- **P**hysically able.
- **O**kay, with Spam, wild animals, and peeing (etc.) in the woods.

Preparation

It's crucial that you do your research before hitting the trail, but more importantly, that you pack the right gear. I strongly recommend that you create and use a checklist to help you remember the important stuff, because if you forget the corkscrew for the wine, you're well—you know. (Then again, the average bottle of wine weighs two pounds, so you'll want to leave that home too.)

The general rule of thumb is that your pack weight shouldn't exceed one-third of your body weight, so you have to be very strategic about what you take. Which reminds me, if you're considering a backpacking trip, and you haven't read or seen Cheryl Strayed's story Wild—you should. Her journey confirmed my worst fears, but my biggest takeaway was this: "Really?! Was the person who sold her that backpack high?" It was *way too big* for her 110-pounds, and, as a result, she ended up packing a lot of stuff she didn't need. In fact, it was so enormous her fellow backpackers nicknamed it "the monster" and teased her every time they crossed paths.

I created this list to give you an idea of what goes into a typical backpack, so read it and weep (I mean, check it out).

<u>*His*</u>

1. Bear bell & spray
2. Bear-resistant food container
3. Cathole trowel (for waste)
4. Clothes
5. Emergency call device
6. Fire starter
7. First aid kit
8. Food
9. Ground cloth
10. Hygiene kit
    - Absorbent pack towel
    - Alcohol gel-based hand sanitizer
    - All-purpose biodegradable soap
    - Bath wipes
    - Cotton bandana or washcloth
    - Dental floss
    - T.P. (or paper towels) in a plastic bag
    - Toothbrush & paste
11. Insect repellent
12. Knife

13. Light source
14. Map & navigation device
15. Mess kit (all-in-one "kitchen kit")
16. Rope
17. Sleeping bag & pad
18. Stove & fuel
19. Sunscreen
20. Tent or tarp
21. Water filter

Yours

1. Backpack
2. Clothes
3. Hygiene kit
   - Same as *His* (plus some)
4. Mirror

I'm kidding. Well, sort of. The key to a successful backpack trip is to distribute the weight as much as possible. To accomplish this, most backpackers go in pairs, or in small groups, but they also travel together for safety. Having said that, Cheryl (played by Reese Witherspoon in the movie) couldn't divvy up the weight because she hiked the Pacific Coast Trail alone.

I'll expand more on gear in Chapter 3, but for now, just know that this form of camping requires thoughtful preparation and a minimalistic mindset.

Physically able

Backpacking isn't for the faint of heart, so you'll also need to be in shape. Ask yourself this question (and be honest): "Can

I hike five miles a day, carrying a 40-pound pack on my back?" And if you think you can because your pedometer logs two miles a day just running errands—think again. Hiking miles are more strenuous than walking miles because you have to exert more energy to traverse them (especially if the trail has a lot of elevation changes and obstacles).

Happily, I've never had to endure this form of torture because my husband knows my limitations. Once upon a time, I considered the idea but came to my senses after witnessing a very distressed Diva and her man in Yosemite. We were on the 16-mile day hike to Half Dome, and they were on what looked like the hike to hell. The trail was steep, rocky, dusty, crowded, hot, and worst of all—long. She was sitting on a rock, clutching her backpack straps, gasping for air, sweating profusely, and shooting death rays at the dude. It wasn't pretty. We passed quickly, but I'll never forget her agony. Clearly, this gal didn't have a clue what awaited her when she set out on *that* trip.

Spam

A few paragraphs back I mentioned that you had better be okay with Spam. I said this because unless you want to backpack with a cooler, you can't take perishable food. So you have a choice, pack things that don't require refrigeration (like Spam, trail mix, granola bars, and jerky). Or, head on down to REI and pick up some of their mush, or freeze-dried meal options, which only require hot water. On second thought, I shouldn't say, "only" because hot water is a real luxury when you're backpacking. In *Wild,* Cheryl (Reese) had to eat cold mush for several days because she had the wrong fuel for her camp stove. (If you've read the book or seen the movie, you know which store sold her the wrong gear, but I'm not going to divulge that information here.) In any case, her cold mush didn't look very appetizing. Apparently Top Ramen is a staple food item for backpackers, but I'll expand on various types of camping cuisine in Chapter 4.

Wild animals

Now, let's talk about the wild things, and where they are. I can't tell you exactly what you'll see during your trek into the wilderness, but I can speak in general terms. I'm a native Californian, and while camping I've encountered bears, deer, turkeys, jackrabbits, raccoons, squirrels, chipmunks, and numerous birds. Although I haven't seen any coyotes, I have laid awake a few summer nights listening to their eerie howls. Luckily, my reptile encounters have been minimal, but I have come across numerous lizards and garter snakes. And although I've had to endure flies and mosquitoes, I hardly ever see spiders. Undoubtedly, your critter encounters will vary from mine, especially if you're not camping in California, but we'll explore this topic more in Chapter 5.

Peeing (etc.) in the woods

Although you can't keep nature from calling when you're backpacking through the boondocks, you can answer the call responsibly. And I'll be honest, sometimes it's not pretty. But it's part of backpacking, so if you decide to engage in this activity, you should abide by the rules. First, avoid peeing on plants if at all possible because critters will destroy them in pursuit of the salty urine you leave behind. Instead, find a rock or hard surface to go on. And, when you have "serious business," find a spot at least 200 feet away from a water source, trail, or your campsite, and dig a six-inch cathole with a trowel. (I'm going to stop here, but if you're curious about what to do next, please see Additional Reading at the back of this book.)

Bathing is part of the, "etc." in "peeing in the woods," and also worthy of reflection. Some backpackers take the motto "Leave No Trace" so seriously they won't even leave soap residue in streams, rivers, or lakes. While I understand that these folks love the environment and want to preserve it for all of eternity, I take a more moderate stance on the issue. Yes, for crying out loud, do take a sponge bath or solar shower, but do it responsibly. The all-purpose biodegradable soap listed a few pages back is a backpacking staple because it cleans everything (your body, clothes, dishes, and hair). I'll discuss specific bath wipes and all-purpose biodegradable soap in Chapter 3, but if you go the bath wipe route, do the planet a favor and pack the used ones out.

CAR CAMPING

This form of camping essentially means you're pitching a tent near your car. And, though I find it a little primitive, it isn't *as* primitive as backpacking. The trick to keeping your misery to a minimum is to choose the right campground, campsite, and gear.

The Good, The Bad, and the Ugly

The Good

Car camping is an activity that *everyone can enjoy* because tents are relatively cheap, and you don't need a truck (i.e., there's nothing to tow). So you can pack up your flashy convertible, practical minivan, or cute little mini cooper for that matter, and hit the road. And since you don't need to plan every single detail, or pull out an RV, you also have the luxury of being more *spontaneous*. Equally important, you have more *freedom* to move about the planet, which means you can set up camp and drive away to escape (I mean, explore!). Or go out to breakfast. Whatever, there's no judgment here.

Tent sites tend to be nicer in the *nature* department than RV sites, but they come at a price—in this case, it's water, and lights. The last time I checked, even the newest, snazziest tents didn't have hookups, so you're stuck using a lantern and hauling your water from the community faucet. But at least you'll have a spacious site to haul it to, and a scenic view as you travel back and forth. If you choose wisely, that is.

The Bad

Most campgrounds have public restrooms, which, generally speaking, are fine, but not always. Sometimes, they are anything but fine. That being said, keep in mind that there are two types: restrooms with pit toilets and restrooms with flush toilets. I've been in both and take it from me; if you have the option, choose a campground with flush toilets. The pit toilets smell terrible. Actually, that's an understatement. But you get my drift.

Another downside to car camping is all the stuff you'll need to make the trip bearable. I've created this list of essential and optional camping gear, etc., to give you an idea of what I mean, but your list could be longer (or shorter).

Car Camping Gear List

ESSENTIAL	OPTIONAL
Bath towels	Acrylic dishes
Collapsible sink	Acrylic wine glasses
Cooler/ice	Air mattress or cot
Dish soap/towels	BBQ grill
Fire starter	Beach towels
First aid kit	Bikes
Food/beverages	Camp chairs
Ground cloth	Citronella
Insect repellent	Coffee maker
Light source	Corkscrew
Paper cups/plates	Dust pan/broom
Paper towels/wipes	Fishing rods
Pillow	Games
Plastic silverware	Hammock
Pots/pans	Mallet
Sleeping bag/pad	Media (iPods, etc.)
Stove	Salt/pepper shakers
Sunscreen	Shade canopy
Tent	Silverware
Trash bags	Trash can
Toiletries	Vinyl tablecloth
Utensils	Watercraft (canoe etc.)

For the record, I should state that all forms of camping require a lot of stuff. The difference is that when you car camp, you have to pack it up every time you go. While, on the contrary, if you have an RV, most of it can be stored inside said RV. I'll expand more on gear needed for car camping in Chapter 3, and packing for children and pets in Chapter 6. Just know that if they come along, you're going to need a U-Haul to carry all their paraphernalia. (But they're worth it.)

The Ugly

Practice setting up that new tent (or the old one if you haven't used it for awhile) at home before you go. I've witnessed many folks trying to juggle instructions, flashlights and their tents in the dark or rain, which is no way to start a camping trip. And avoid low areas when you choose your spot because rainwater travels downhill and will collect underneath your tent. Also, whatever you do, don't skip the rainfly! If you put it on correctly, you'll still be ventilated but protected from leaks. And finally, bring a little mat to wipe your feet off before you climb in—otherwise they'll be so much dirt inside you might as well sleep outside.

POP-UP CAMPERS (aka tent trailers)

You don't have to pee in the woods or share a public restroom that looks like Mama, Papa, *and* Baby Bear just left. And forget about sleeping on the ground. Diva, in my mind, this camping option is the perfect compromise. They're way more comfortable than a traditional tent, but not as luxurious as a trailer or motor home. Also, they're easy to store, easy to tow, are allowed in most campgrounds and—best of all—have a "kitchen" and "restroom."

A pop-up consists of a trailer frame, a hard roof, pull-out beds, soft walls made of canvas, and vinyl windows with screens. When collapsed, the average pop-up is 12 feet long, but they double in size when open. The beauty of them is that they allow you to see the beauty around you, well, without letting in the bugs. When the curtains are open, they offer a 360-degree view that you're not going to get in a tent, trailer, or motor home. Another benefit worth mentioning is the fact that pop-up campers are elevated (usually 36 inches) off the ground. It may not seem like a huge thing; however, the divide between you and the dirt might as well be Mount Everest in the eyes of most critters. Also, because they have actual doors, the natural tendency is to close them, but you can forget to zip up your tent. I've heard stories about all kinds of critters getting into the unsuspecting camper's tent. And they're not all cute. I'm talking snakes. And bears. Need I say more?

There are two types of pop-ups, standard, and high-wall. The main difference between the two is the high wall pop-ups have more aluminum and less canvas. (Making residential height countertops and more storage space possible.) They all have comfortable sleeping areas, little dinettes, refrigerators, sinks, and stoves, but most high wall pop-ups have a whole lot more. We're talking heaters, air conditioners, dual sinks, ovens, microwaves, surround sound, and best of all, walls around the bathroom.

And last, but certainly not least, pop-ups have running water, gas, and lights. Whether you're "plugged" or "unplugged" (i.e., boondocking), these luxuries will not only make your experience bearable, but fun. Sure, you could rub two sticks together and build a fire outside, but why would you when you can accomplish the same thing from inside the safe, bug free shelter of your pop-up?

TRAILER CAMPING

The trailer. Where should I begin? I guess I should start by saying that there are many different types, in many different sizes. Some are compact and can go almost everywhere; others are enormous and can hardly go anywhere. We upgraded from our beloved high wall pop-up to a trailer for the following reasons:

1. It's bear proof.
2. It's climate controlled.
3. It's more convenient.

Don't get me wrong, we've got nothing against bears. In fact, they're pretty darn cute. But as I said, they smell, and although bears are rarely aggressive toward humans, they are aggressive in their pursuit of food. So, let me ask you this: If canvas is the only thing separating a bear from food, who do you think will win? In fact, many campgrounds don't even allow tents or pop-ups in grizzly bear country (Alaska, Idaho, Montana, Washington, and Wyoming).

Pop-ups have a lot of good qualities, but insulation is not one of them (which is fine if you only camp in the summer). However, if you want to visit Yosemite or Yellowstone during the fall or spring, you might get a tad chilly. And forget about snow camping in a pop-up; you and your Tarzan could quite possibly freeze to death, even *if* you crawl into the same sleeping bag and cling to each other for dear life.

And finally, setting up a pop-up and then breaking it down can be time-consuming. They typically take around 25 to 35 minutes to set up, and if you clean it before you break it down, it'll take longer. But don't worry, if necessary, it's possible to collapse and hitch up in 10 minutes flat. (I know this because a forest fire chased us out of our campground once.)

So, now that I've established the three major benefits of camping in a trailer, let me touch on some of the other pros (and cons) related to owning or renting one.

Pros: Trailer vs. Pop-Up Camper

Size

Size can be a pro *and* a con. The reason: although most trailers are bigger than a pop-up, what you gain in amenities, you lose in scenery. Does that sound familiar? I said the exact opposite about car camping. Because of this, we ended up choosing a small, but "mighty" trailer when it was time to upgrade so that we could still visit our favorite campgrounds. For example, DL Bliss in Lake Tahoe has a maximum trailer length of 18 feet, which, not coincidentally, is the length of our trailer.

Bathroom

Having a bathroom equipped with a sink is one of the biggest differences between a pop-up and a trailer. Confused? Well, pop-ups only have one sink, which means you're spitting your toothpaste into the same place that you're washing your dishes. On the other hand, a trailer has two, one in the "bathroom," and one in the "kitchen." In my opinion, having access to a private bathroom (sink or not) is a luxury that can make or break a camping trip. I think I've explained this one enough so I won't go into any more detail. Just trust me, there's nothing romantic about squatting in the woods or stumbling to the bathroom in the middle of the night. I don't care if the moon *is* full!

Kitchen

Most trailers have larger refrigerators and freezers than pop-ups, which is particularly useful if you're planning to camp longer than two days. We loved our pop-up but had to take two coolers to store perishables, because everything wouldn't fit in our little refrigerator. Which wasn't the end of the world; however, I don't miss the frequent trips to the bear box. (But alas, I'm getting ahead of myself. I discuss bear boxes in Chapter 5.)

Storage (of your stuff)

Another benefit worth mentioning is storage. Although we had two "bedrooms" in our pop-up, the one we didn't sleep in became the "junk room" for all our stuff. Which meant every time we needed clothes, we had to crawl up on the bed to get to them. On the other hand, our trailer is much more convenient because it has a nice little closet that allows us to hang stuff up, with drawers for everything else. After all, where is it written that just because you're camping, you should look like you've slept in your clothes?

Television

Again, I think this feature falls in both the pro and con categories. Although I enjoy getting away from it all, I also like watching an occasional movie if we're camping for an extended period. Most trailers come equipped with some form of television (ours is a 19-inch flat screen that attaches to the wall and swings out). On the flip side, if a television is the deciding factor when choosing a trailer, then maybe camping isn't your thing. Seriously, Diva, you can watch *Project Runway* at home. Do you really need to see who's made what when you're camping under the stars?

Cons: Trailer vs. Pop-Up Camper

Cost

Generally speaking, trailers are more expensive than pop-ups, so you'll need to decide how much you want one, and how much you're willing to spend. They range in price (between $2,000 and $20,000), depending on the age, size, and features. Other costs to consider when purchasing a trailer are insurance, registration, and storage.

Towing

But if you do decide to purchase a trailer, make sure your truck or SUV has enough horsepower to pull it. You'd be surprised to learn how many people forget to consider this *tiny little detail.*

A friend of mine used to own a 24-foot Prowler, but her little truck could barely tow the darn thing. The gist of this story is she pissed off a lot of people going up hills. It was stressful for her, not to mention her fellow travelers. Check your car manual before you purchase, bearing in mind that an acceptable "tow rating" for your vehicle is at least 25% higher than the loaded weight of your trailer.

Storage (of your trailer)

Unless you live in the country, or on a gigantic lot, you'll have to pay to store your trailer somewhere. Our old pop-up used to fit in the garage, but our new trailer doesn't, so we pay $75 a month to store it. We use it a lot, so it's worth it to us, but you should consider this cost before making a purchase. If you don't camp enough to justify the expense, then maybe renting is a better option for you.

TRUCK CAMPERS

The truck camper sort of reminds me of a turtle. I'm not saying they're slow, but campers and turtles both move about with their shells attached, and provide shelter when they're sleeping. Some are very basic; others tricked out. Talk about small, but mighty—some of the newer campers have everything a pop-up or trailer has, but on a smaller scale in much less space. Put it this way: a New Yorker would feel right at home in one of these babies. Having said that, all truck campers—old and new, have a bed over the cab, and their shells are removable.

16

A truck camper isn't a bad option because they offer the best of both worlds: wheels *and* shelter. You and Tarzan can still explore the jungle around you because it's small enough to drive around, and it's relatively easy to set up and break down. You just pull in, set your break and stabilizers, put blocks behind the tires, pull down the stairs, and push the slide out button (assuming you have a slide out). You'll also need to set up your camp with chairs, hammock, and tablecloth, etc.—but all that stuff can stay behind if you want to drive away for a few hours. Some people who camp for extended periods of time choose to unhook their camper shells and anchor them in their campsite much like regular trailer owners do. I should state, though that some campers are easier than others to unhitch, and that I've only seen the newer models solo.

So if you think this form of camping is right for you, keep in mind that campers and trucks aren't always compatible. It's best to purchase the shell first if you don't already own a truck because it's easier to find the truck to fit your dream camper shell than vice versa.

MOTOR HOME CAMPING

Friends of ours used to own a super big, super slick, 35-foot motor home, but we rarely got to camp with them because it exceeded the maximum length at our favorite campgrounds. So if we wanted to camp with them, we had to "cross over to the other side," the RV park side that is. Here's the thing, sometimes RV parks have more in common with parking lots than campgrounds. Not always, but they're out there, so just beware. We visited one such park not too long ago, and they had an area called "The Cliff." The running joke for the weekend became: "Yeah, they call it 'The Cliff' because if you end up there, you'll want to jump off one!" Oh, good times, good times!

On the other hand, in defense of these traveling homes, a true Diva will think she's died and gone to heaven because most of these rigs are downright luxurious. In fact, some of them are nicer than some people's homes. And, the RV parks that house them offer full hookups, not to mention amenities like swimming pools, convenience stores, and laundry facilities. So if you want to commune with nature, without giving up the comforts of home, then this "camping" option is definitely for you.

While we're on the subject, there are three motor home classes, and in case you're curious, they are:

Class A

Our friends' 35-foot motor home was a Class A. They resemble a bus and are the largest RV on the market (up to 45 feet). But if you're considering renting or purchasing one, you should know that these vehicles come with a hefty price tag ($119,000 on average). They also cost a small fortune to gas up ($250 on average). *Cha-ching!!!* Jeez, for that amount of money I could buy a designer handbag. Or better yet, get a room.

Class B

These vehicles look like a minivan and are very similar to the camper as far as size and functionality go, minus the over-the-cab bed. Again, the older models are pretty basic, but the newer ones are packed full of features, including a little kitchen and bathroom. Regardless, we're talking tight quarters here. The average Class B is 18 feet long, so if you have a family, this probably isn't an option for you. And at the risk of stating the obvious again, this also applies to campers.

Class C

This class resembles a camper because of their over-the-cab beds, but they're larger (25 feet on average). I think of them as the "mama bears" of the motor home family. They're not too small and not too big…they're *just* right. Spacious enough to accommodate more than you and your man, but not so big that you can't maneuver the darn thing. Also noteworthy is the fact that they're fuel-efficient. (I don't know about you, but I'd rather not spend all of my vacation money on gas.)

GLAMPING

Although it takes on many forms, this camping option mostly means *glamorous camping*. I love the word glamping because it conjures up so many fun images. Like bellmen setting up elaborate tents or a hot rock treatment in a stream, or—better yet—a claw-foot tub in the middle of the woods. Well, you probably won't find a massage table in a stream or a tub in the woods. But you could quite possibly find a spa within a glampground, or a company to set up your campsite.

Speaking of which, *Adventure in Camping* (Mammoth Lakes, CA), and *Acker RV Rentals* (Lake Tahoe, NV), will do just that.

Both companies pack, tow, set up, and break down one of their trailers for you. All you have to do is choose one from their easy-to-navigate websites, pay for it, and show up. Their prices are reasonable, and since they're in the business of camping, you'll get professional advice about which campground and campsite best fit your needs. There are other companies who provide the same service, but sorry; you're going to have to Google it because I couldn't find a one-stop, national source.

If you decide to get your glamp on, you can do it in a variety of ways. Try renting a safari tent, a hut, a tipi, a yurt, a treehouse, or a vintage Airstream trailer. (Bearing in mind, of course, that some glampgrounds have more amenities than others.) On the low end, you'll find a bug free space that has electricity, actual beds, rustic furnishings, nearby dining options, and shared bathrooms. On the high end, you'll find comfy beds with Egyptian cotton sheets, plush towels and rugs, stylish furnishings, flat-screen televisions, room service, fine dining, Jacuzzis, and spas. I could go on, but you get the idea. *Glamping.com* and *GlampingHub.com* manage reservations for this fun new craze, so if this is something that appeals to you, then by all means, check them out. (I was impressed.)

Before I move on to my next topic, let me leave you with this thought. Although we camp in a trailer, I like to think we're glamping because our trailer is really nice, we only camp in premium spots, and we have all the right gear. But more importantly, we always squeeze in at least one dinner in a restaurant or at the very least, cocktails on a scenic deck. Even so, the fact that we don't camp with hookups might disqualify us in the minds of some Divas. No matter—as I said before, it's a relative term, so whatever type of camping you decide to tackle, do it with style and—glamping accomplished!

A Word About Boondocking

Nope, I'm not talking about that remote place commonly referred to as the "boondocks." I'm talking about the expression used to describe camping in an RV *without hookups*. Some campgrounds sell electricity, water, and sewer access via said hookups, but if you're staying in a campground that doesn't offer them, you have to *boondock* it.

Essentially this means a battery runs your lights, a holding tank holds your water, and you have to empty your sewer. (Which, personally I don't think is a big deal, you just have to remember to turn off the lights and take short showers.) That said, you should know that batteries and holding tanks vary in size and should be a consideration when renting or purchasing—especially if you plan to camp for more than a few days.

The longest we've ever camped is six nights, and we had to fill up the water tank three times, empty the gray water (dish and shower) twice, and the sewer once. I should warn you, however, that some RVs are easier than others to fill and or drain. For example, our high wall pop-up had a toilet cartridge that slid in and out for easy disposal, but our snazzy new trailer doesn't have such a cartridge; the tank is stationary. For this reason, we purchased a plastic holding tank on wheels for long trips, which essentially accomplishes the same goal.

So, if all of this scares the crap out of you (pun intended), make sure that your campground of choice has hookups! I don't mind boondocking Diva, but I'll be honest—sometimes I do yearn for a long shower, especially after bushwhacking my way through the jungle.

Light My Fire

When it's time to build a campfire, be smart about it. Make sure there's no debris around the fire ring that could catch fire, never leave it unattended, and have plenty of water on hand to douse the fire. (Especially if you burn out before it does.) Also, do not, under any circumstances use white gas to speed up the process. Instead, build a little teepee with your softwood (pine, fir and cedar work best), and light it with a long-necked fire starter. Then, once your fire is at a respectable blaze, throw on some hardwood, to keep it going. (Softwood ignites quickly, but hardwood burns longer.) For more information on this subject, see Additional Reading at the back of this book.

Renting an RV

Diva, there's a reason there are so many "barely used" RVs for sale on Craigslist, so before you plunk money down on one, I strongly recommend that you rent a few first. That said, you can rent all of the recreational vehicles we've reviewed in this chapter, though I should caution you that some are easier than others to find. If you're interested in a pop-up camper, you'll have to Google them because there isn't a national supplier. But, if you'd like to rent a trailer or motor home, go to *CruiseAmerica*.

com (for Class Cs) or *ElMonteRV.com* (for Class As, Class Cs, and trailers).

The most popular RV rental is the Class C. I'm not an authority on the subject, but I would venture to say this is due, in part, to the reasons already stated. (Size, maneuverability, and fuel efficiency.) Also, you don't have to tow a Class C, which means you don't need a truck or SUV to enjoy this type of camping. They range in price, but the average rental fee is $155+ per day. In addition to the base price, they also charge a deposit, tax, and for fuel.

CHAPTER 1 TIPS

✓ Don't forget to tell someone exactly where you're going and when you'll be back before you head into the wilderness! That way, if you don't return when you're supposed to, a search party will know where to look.

✓ If a thunderstorm rolls in, take shelter in your car with the windows up. The "Faraday cage" effect (not your rubber tires), will shield you from lightening strikes.

✓ Consider what your view will be when you open your tent, trailer, or motor home door, and if possible, plan accordingly.

✓ Generally speaking, campgrounds "quiet times" are from 10 PM to 6 AM, so keep it down unless you want a visit from the camp host or ranger.

✓ Work out those hand signals with the driver before he or she attempts to back that trailer or motor home into your campsite.

Two

Campgrounds & Sites:
Booking Your Accommodations

August 9, 1999
Suburban L.A. (on the edge of reason)
When the website described the campground as having "scenic views," I sincerely hope it wasn't referring to our oh-so-close-hillbilly neighbors.

My second camping experience with my Tarzan wasn't as terrible as the first, but it wasn't good. We stayed in an enormous, mostly asphalt campground, flanked by dusty little campsites. It had zero trees and, therefore, no privacy. We could practically reach out and touch our fellow campers, but believe me, this is never a good thing. Brad Pitt doesn't camp. At least not in the destinations we frequent. The best feature about this particular campground was the fact that we could leave, which we did. We took a short drive to a charming little lake and had a delicious picnic lunch in a rented rowboat. It was a warm, sunny day, and this excursion made up for the asphalt jungle's shortfalls.

The lesson here? Do your research before you book your accommodations. Of course, if all you need is a place to lay your head, then pitching your tent any ol' where is perfectly fine, as long as your goal is just to sleep and not camp.

Campsite Finders

I understand that booking your accommodations can be daunting, but there are websites available to help you sort through all the information. *ReserveAmerica.com* is an excellent place to start and functions a lot like *Hotels.com*. Simply plug in your destination, dates, site type, and—voila!—available campgrounds and sites meeting your criteria magically appear. For example, Reserve America's home page asks the following questions with dropdowns to help narrow your search:

Find an adventure
Where?
>   Enter a location

Interested in:
- Everything
- Camping & Lodging
- Day use & Picnic areas

Looking for:
- Any camp spot
- RV sites
- Trailer sites
- Tent
- Cabins or lodgings
- Group sites
- Day use

- Horse sites
- Boat sites

Camping Dates (Specific, or Range) _____

Arrival Dates _____

Length of Stay _____

This screen is fairly simple to follow; you click on one of the bullet options and fill in the blanks. To refine your search even further, click on "More Options" if you're looking for something specific (i.e., handicap, waterfront, pet-friendly, or electrical hookup sites).

Another good source for researching and booking your camping trip is *Recreation.gov*. It works pretty much the same way, but they only manage reservations for Federal and State campgrounds (etc.), hence the .gov at the end of their domain. I like *recreation.gov* because their website has photos of individual campsites, and they have an advance check-in system. (Which is nice when you have anxious children or dogs jumping around on the back seat.)

I'm old school and haven't jumped onto the app bandwagon yet, but if you have, then check out *ALLSTAYS Camp & RV*. It's a highly rated camping app created by campers for campers that features over 25,950 US and Canadian campgrounds and RV parks. It functions with or without Internet access (although you'll need it for the map feature), and its superior filters only display relevant information. In addition to highlighting all types of campgrounds, it also locates overnight parking lots, rest areas, RV dealers, RV service providers, and RV rental locations, just to name a few. It costs $10 and runs on all Apple devices (iOS 4.3 or later). But don't panic Android users, it also runs on your phone with a minimum requirement of 2.1 and up.

The *We Camp Here* app for Android users (2.2 and up) is less expensive at $4, but doesn't have all the camping related service locators that ALLSTAYS does. Still, it's a solid campsite finder app that has a personal campground organizer feature, allowing you to save your favorite campsites in a cloud by clicking on the "My Campgrounds" button. It's also easy to navigate and has a high rating.

Your destination is half the journey

Deciding on a destination for your camping trip (i.e., Yosemite or Lake Tahoe, etc.) is the easy part. Finding the best campground and campsite within one of these national treasures is a little trickier. To help narrow your search, consider the following before clicking on "book this site:"

1. Proximity to civilization
2. Proximity to the highway
3. Proximity to recreation
4. Campground size
5. Campground type
6. Campsite location
7. Amenities

The campground size, type, location, and amenities are pretty obvious, but you'll need to dig a little deeper to determine how close it is to civilization, the highway, and recreation.

Proximity to civilization

It's important to know where the closest town is before you commit to a camping trip, in case you need to find an urgent care or hospital. Now, *how* close is up to you, but personally, I'm comfortable within a 30-mile radius. It's far enough away from the hustle and bustle, but not so close that I might as well get a room. Also, it's nice to know that there's a store nearby in case you forget the wine—I mean, butter!

Proximity to the highway

If you'd rather listen to crickets than traffic, you'll want to check the distance from the campground to the highway. You might as well get a room in the big city if the noise of passing cars doesn't bother you. Recently, I spent a couple of nights car camping in Fort Bragg, California, and although the campground was only 100 feet from the beach; my campsite butted up against a bluff with the highway above. I was so worried that a car was going to crash through the flimsy wood fence and crush me—I barely slept.

There are campgrounds in Lake Tahoe that fit in this category, but I'm not going to name them (because I believe in karma). Some are 10 feet from the highway. So picture this: you wake up, stretch, rub your eyes, slip on your slippers, and step outside to take in the glorious surroundings. But instead of said surroundings, the first thing you see is an SUV full of gawking eyes. No. Thank. You. But, if you must, make sure you pack your cute pajamas if you plan to camp in one of these campgrounds.

Proximity to recreation

As stated briefly in the introduction of this chapter, your recreation options are also important. Unless, of course, you have a spacious campsite with beautiful views, and you just want to veg out. I'm groovy with that, but what you don't want is to be stuck in an overly crowded campground with nothing but a weed separating you and your neighbor. Nonetheless, if this is your only option, make sure you have something fun to do away from your actual campsite. Look for a lake with watercraft rentals so that you can canoe, paddleboard, kayak, water ski, or fish—whatever floats your boat. Or, if recreating on the water isn't your thing, look for hiking trails, or, if you prefer, shops and restaurants. My husband and I like to have it all: a nice campsite *and* plenty of recreational opportunities nearby. That's just how we roll. We're not good vegging out at our campsite, no matter how nice it is.

Campground size

Pay attention to the total number of campsites within the campground. I'm not saying that small vs. large is better or worse, but more campsites equal more campers and, therefore, more *noise.* However, on the plus side, large campgrounds tend to have more amenities like sewer dump stations, flush toilets, showers, and amphitheaters. And no—camp hosts don't show actual movies at these amphitheaters; they're mostly used by rangers to educate campers about the local animals and landscape. Or for sing-alongs. So if you're into singing *Kumbayah* with strangers, you'll feel right at home at one of these campgrounds.

Campground type

For the most part, there are four different types of campgrounds: *federal, state, private,* and *other* (usually managed by a county or water district). I won't bore you too much with specifics here, but you should know that federal and state campgrounds tend to be stricter than private and other campgrounds. And I'd like to tell you that each type has distinct characteristics, but it's not that simple. All four come in various sizes and varieties, with different amenities, rules, and regulations.

Having said that, there are certain types of campgrounds, which attract certain types of people. At the risk of profiling, I think it's safe to say that seniors tend to frequent *RV Parks,* families tend to frequent *KOA parks,* and long-term campers tend to frequent *RV Resorts.* Now, I'm not saying that you won't cross paths with a senior citizen or a family at a state or federal campground because you will. I'm just saying they tend to frequent RV Parks and KOAs. You'll encounter a more eclectic group of people at the government owned and managed campgrounds, whereas the privately owned campgrounds tend to cater to a particular demographic.

Campsite location

Okay, so you've finally picked your campground. Yay! Now, assuming you've checked the campground's location and recreation options; as well as the hookup or restroom situations—you're ready to choose your site.

The next thing, you should do, is click on the campsite map. Take a good look at the sample on the next page, notice anything? Some things are pretty obvious...others, not so much. Here's what I see:

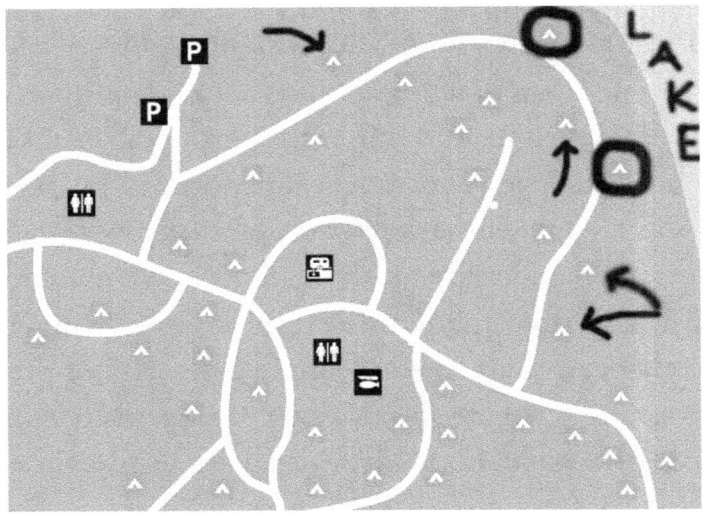

The obvious

There are around 40 campsites in this particular campground loop, some being larger than others. Only a few are lakeside, but some probably offer a partial lake view. Additionally, there's a station for cleaning fish, another for pumping sewer, two restrooms, and two overflow parking lots.

The not so obvious

Personally, I'd avoid the campsites near fish guts and sewer; nevertheless, because these stations are somewhat segregated, they're hardly a concern here. Likewise, these restrooms are off the beaten path, but sometimes they're tucked between campsites. They tend to generate a lot of traffic though, so if you'd rather avoid it, pay attention to where they are. Most campgrounds only allow two vehicles per campsite, so the overflow parking lots will come in handy if you're planning to park more than two. (A trailer is classified as a vehicle in this context.) And since the idea of being in a fish bowl doesn't appeal to me, I would also stay away from the interior sites situated inside of the squiggly lines (i.e., roads). Often, they have fewer trees and can leave you feeling a little exposed, but not always.

I've pointed to the good campsites and circled the best, but because there are no actual photos in this sample, I'm making an educated guess. Still, these maps are a helpful tool and should be considered before you book any site.

We use *ReserveAmerica.com* 95% of the time because they manage most of the campgrounds we frequent, and their website is easy to navigate. For example, when you hover over a tent symbol, the campsite information pops up. Referring to the previous map sample, this is what you'll see if you hover over the circled tent symbol in the upper right-hand corner:

Site: **127**

Loop: **Two**

Site Type: **Standard**

Driveway Surface: **Paved**

Driveway Entry: **Back In**

Max Vehicle Length: **71**

Shade: **Partial**

Site Rating: **Developed**

Again, this is fairly simple to follow, but I'll point out the less obvious stuff. A lot of campgrounds have more than one group of sites (i.e. loops); the campground in this sample has four. For the most part, there are two types of sites: Standard or Group, which is telling you how many people are allowed per site. This particular campground allows eight people in their standard sites and 40 in their group sites. Typically the driveways are paved, but not always. Likewise, most are of the back-in variety. If there's only one thing you pay attention to when you hover over one of these sites, it should be the *max vehicle length*. It's not rocket science, but if your rig won't *fit*, then neither will you and all your stuff. And lastly, "developed" usually means there's a fire ring, picnic table, a water source nearby, and—in bear country—a bear box.

Amenities

You won't find any campgrounds that offer robes or a Heavenly bed, but some do have pools, general stores, laundry rooms, and playgrounds, among other things. Amenities vary wildly, depending on the type of campground that you choose, but this list should give you an idea of what to look for at least.

Other/Small Campgrounds

1. Fire rings
2. Picnic table
3. Restrooms
4. Water nearby

State/Federal Campgrounds

1. ADA access
2. Amphitheatre

3. Bear boxes
4. Bicycle riding
5. Boating
6. Fire rings
7. Firewood
8. Fishing
9. Group camping
10. Hiking trails
11. Host
12. Kiosk (check-in)
13. Overflow parking
14. Picnic tables
15. Restrooms
16. Sewer dump stations
17. Showers
18. Swimming
19. Water nearby

RV Resorts/KOA Campgrounds

1. ADA access
2. Amphitheatre
3. Fire rings (sometimes)
4. General store
5. Hookups (water, electrical, sewer)
6. Host
7. Kiosk (check-in)
8. Laundry facilities
9. Overflow parking

10. Picnic tables
11. Playground
12. Restrooms
13. Sewer dump stations
14. Showers
15. Swimming pool

CHAPTER 2 TIPS

- ✓ If you want to visit a particular campground, figure out what the booking window is, and call or click "book this site" the first minute they go on sale. (Our favorite campsites sell out in **5** minutes during peak season.)

- ✓ Again, some campgrounds don't allow tents or pop-ups in grizzly bear country, so if you're planning to camp in Alaska, Idaho, Montana, Washington, and Wyoming, check before you go.

- ✓ Don't choose a site near standing water if mosquitoes like to suck your blood.

- ✓ Pay attention to how much shade the campsite has if you're sensitive to the sun (or you're a sun worshipper).

- ✓ Keep in mind that the host is there to maintain order, so being in proximity could be good or bad, depending on how you look at it.

Three

Clothing, Gear, & Products

July 23, 2002
Big Bear Lake, CA
   ARGH! I lost more marshmallows to the blazing beast tonight. Total roasting attempts made: too many to count. Total edible results for consumption: zero.

Okay Diva, you know how a pair of shoes or that perfect little black dress, can make or break an event? If you choose wisely, your wardrobe choices can help attract that guy you have a crush on or better yet, help you land that big job. Well, what you wear is also important when recreating outdoors. And I'm not just talking about temperature appropriate clothing here; I'm talking about things you probably wouldn't even consider.

Think seriously about what you're going to do away from your campsite, and plan accordingly. If you're planning to hike, you should wear comfortable, loose-fitting, breathable shorts, not tight-fitting bike shorts. I'm embarrassed to say that I did this once. Talk about "too much information," I still feel sorry for the poor folks who were behind us on *that* hiking trail.

Another time, I wore a sleeveless tank top because it was hot outside, and almost had to be airlifted out of a canyon with heat exhaustion. The hike down was fine but by the time we turned around to retrace our steps, I was dehydrated, disoriented, and stumbling. Gone was my fear of bumping into snakes; on the way up, all I wanted to do was lie down and curl up with them. I'm not joking that was a scary day. Have you ever noticed people who work outdoors in the heat, wear long sleeves and a hat? I know this defies logic; however, the same principle that keeps us warm, also tends to keep us cool.

CLOTHING

Athleta, REI, Sports Authority, and *Title Nine* have a great selection of clothing for outdoor activities. Did you know, for example, that they sell pants that zip off at the knee and become shorts? Well, they do, and they're great for backpackers, day hikers, and regular campers too. They also sell breathable, moisture wicking garments designed for specific activities to keep you warm or cool (and when appropriate, dry).

Layering

Because temperatures rise with the sun, and your body warms up with exercise, it's important that you dress in layers before setting out on a strenuous hike. You could very well end the day with just one, but you should start out wearing three. In short, they are: *base layer* (against your skin), manages moisture; *insulating layer,* keeps you warm, and *shell layer* (outer), blocks the wind and the rain.

So, for example, you'll want to wear a breathable short-sleeved tee that wicks away moisture, a warm but lightweight fleece sweatshirt, and a weatherproof outer shell over that. And again, your shorts or pants should be breathable, durable, and loose-fitting.

Footwear

Closed Toed/ Closed Heeled Shoes

I used to take sandals and flip-flops when we camped, but I spent so much time cleaning my feet before I went into our trailer, I finally gave up on them. Besides, they're just not practical or safe maneuvering those dirty, sharp and sometimes hot campsite obstacles. I still pack a pair in case we have plans away from our campsite; however, for the most part, I wear running shoes or hiking boots. But watch out, I've singed my share of rubber soles in front of the campfire resting them on the metal fire ring. Still, better rubber soles than your cute little sandals.

Gaiters

Backpackers often wear gaiters over their hiking boots and lower pant legs to help keep snow, water, dirt, and pebbles out. Which is, reason enough to purchase some, but they also prevent ticks etc., from climbing up their pant legs. They come in different lengths, sizes, and types, depending on activity level and the elements.

Hiking Boots

A lot of people end up taking some form of a hike when they camp, because, well, it's a natural progression. So if you plan to tackle anything more strenuous than the paved path to the restroom (or you're going on a backpacking trip), then you're gong to need a good pair of hiking boots.

Regular tennis or running shoes are better than sandals but won't prevent a sprain if you stumble. That's the beauty of the hiking boot—they're designed to support the ankle. But when you're at the store trying them on, make sure you choose water-proof boots that have a little wiggle room to accommodate the thick socks that go inside them. (More on this in a minute.) The person who sold Cheryl her boots failed to tell her this, and, as a result, she ended up losing a few toenails.

Rubber Flip-Flops

Unless you have access to a private shower, you're going to need a pair of rubber flip-flops to maneuver that public shower. Take it from me, you do not want to stand in one of those things *barefooted*; it's just not sanitary. (Unless, of course, you don't mind a little foot fungus.) But if you do, bring the dang flip-flops; they're cheap and easy to pack. Seriously, you'll thank me later.

Socks

These comfy little foot garments will keep your feet clean during the day and warm at night. I always pack more socks than I need because I've learned the hard way that if my feet are dirty, the rest of my body feels dirty, too. And when we hit the trail for a long hike, I always wear two pairs if I forget to pack a thick pair for hiking. Serious backpackers often wear liner socks (that wick away moisture) beneath a pair of thicker socks (usually wool) to help prevent blisters. Also, the added cushion from thick socks just feels better inside those hiking boots.

Hats, Etc.

I'd like to dedicate this paragraph to my friend, Julie, who upon review of my car camping section, said, "Don't forget to mention the importance of the *ball cap*." She's so funny—as *if* I could! Here's the thing: that "good hair day" you have when you set up camp won't last. By day two, you'll be chanting, "Mirror, mirror, on the wall, who's the fairest of them all?" and it won't be you. Personally, I'm a big fan of ball caps because they disguise bad hair *and* look cute on almost everyone.

On the other hand, if a ball cap isn't your thing, consider a *beanie, bandana, cadet cap, straw hat, sun hat,* or *visor.* Vanity aside, these caps and hats are also practical. A beanie will keep your head and ears warm in cold weather; a bandana can double as a washcloth or sweatband, and the hats and caps will help protect against harmful UVA and UVB rays.

Outerwear
Cotton Sweatshirts

I live in my cotton sweatshirts when we camp, so I pack a few because it tends to be chilly in the mornings and the evenings. And, in addition to being cute *and* warm, they're machine washable, which is key because they're going to get dirty. I take a pullover and a zip-up, but prefer the latter because pulling a sweatshirt over a ball-capped head can be tricky.

Down Jackets

Considered by many to be Mother Nature's best insulator, down jackets are warmer, lighter, more compressible, and retain their shape better than synthetic. But, unfortunately, they lose their insulating powers when wet, and take a long time to dry. Another drawback is the fact that it's expensive. However, if you take care of your down jacket, it'll last forever. (Well, not *forever*, but you know what I mean.)

Fleece Jackets, etc.

Fleece is a synthetic fabric created for outdoor enthusiasts who recreate in cold weather and is a must for backpackers. It's soft, durable, reasonably lightweight, quick drying, warm, and inexpensive. You'll find this super fabric in mittens, hats, scarves, sweatshirts, and jackets, but don't expect these garments to keep you dry in a rainstorm because they're not water resistant.

Waterproof Shells/Jackets

Waterproof shells and jackets come in a variety of options ranging in breathability, warmth, weight, durability, flexibility, comfort, versatility, and, of course, water resistance. Generally speaking, there are two materials used to make waterproof jackets, laminate *(Gore-Tex)* and coatings *(HyVent)*, which is a *North Face* brand. Both will keep you dry, but Gore-Tex jackets are more expensive because they're also more breathable.

Like North Face, *Patagonia* and *Marmot* also sell coating brands, but Gore-Tex *is* a brand and for sale on their website, at *Cabela's, LL Bean,* and *REI* (etc.). That said, a coating jacket is fine for summer backpackers and day hikers, but if you're planning to backpack year round at high elevations, then you're going to need a Gore-tex jacket.

Underwear

You should probably ditch the sexy thongs when you backpack or camp, Diva, and pack some cute *boy shorts* or *hipster briefs*, instead. *Patagonia* and *Under Armour* has a good selection of sports bras and stretchy underwear for women that breathe well and, best of all, won't ride up your booty. And they're cute. (I wouldn't lie to you.)

There's some confusion about which *long underwear* or "long johns" are better, thermal or silk. After exhaustive research, I'm happy to say both keep you warm, but silk is better for active people. Don't get me wrong, thermals serve a purpose too… mainly to keep you toasty warm while you sleep, or while you sip hot chocolate by the fire.

GEAR

You're going to need a lot of stuff to survive the elements, and guess what? Camping gear isn't interchangeable. For example, the only thing a backpackers' and car campers' stove has in common is they cook food. An experienced car camper wouldn't attempt to cook for a crowd on a backpacking stove, and vice versa; a backpacker wouldn't carry a regular camp stove in their backpack. So, at the risk of sending you screaming into the woods, I've compiled a table that lists the appropriate gear needed for each camping scenario, followed by a brief description of each item. (D = Definitely, P = Probably, and M = Maybe.)

GEAR, ETC.	BACK PACKERS	CAR CAMPERS	RV CAMPERS
Absorbent pack towel	D	M	
Air mattress or cot		P	
Backpacking pack	D		
BBQ grill		P	M
Bear bell	P	M	M
Bear resistant food container	P		
Bear spray	P	M	M
Cathole trowel	D	M	
Chair	M	D	D
Coffee maker	P	P	P
Cooler		D	P
Daypack		P	M
Dishes		D	D
Dust pan/broom		D	M
Emergency gear	D	P	M
Fire starter	D	D	D
First aid kit	D	D	D
Games		P	P
Generator		P	M
Ground cloth	D	D	
Hammock	M	P	M
Knife	D	P	M
Light source	D	D	D
Mallet		P	M
Map/Navigation device	D	P	M
Mess kit	D		
Pillow	M	D	D
Rope	D	P	M
Shade canopy		D	P
Sink	M	D	
Sleeping bag	D	D	M
Sleeping pad	D	M	
S'mores grill		D	P
Solar shower/shelter	P	M	
Stove	D	D	M
Tent or tarp	D	D	
Trash can/bags	D	D	D
Vinyl tablecloth		P	P
Walking (trekking) poles	P	M	M
Water filters	D	P	M
Wine glasses, etc.		M	M

Retail Outlets

I spent over eighty hours researching the gear and products for this chapter, so I feel as though I have a pretty good handle on what's what. That being said, in the spirit of disclosure, I should state that although I spent a fair amount of time on *REI's* website, the majority was spent on *Amazon* and *Campmor's*.

All three retailers sell similar stuff and have online stores, so if you prefer shopping from the comfort of your home, then check out their websites. Then again, if you're the type of person who has to touch something before you buy it, then by all means, head on down to your local REI (assuming your town has one). Campmor and REI have flexible return policies, excellent customer service and offer free shipping for most items, but Amazon's shipping and return policy varies depending upon the actual seller.

GEAR FOR BACKPACKERS
Absorbent Pack Towel

I was a little skeptical about these towels until I did the research, but their microfiber construction makes them perfect for backpacking because they're super absorbent, quick-drying and reusable. I like the *Sea to Summit Large Tek Towel* for these reasons, and because they're luxurious and pack up small. Campmor customers give them a 4.8 rating, and they sell for $27.

Backpacking Packs

There are a lot of nifty packs on the market these days, but choose wisely. Mostly, you'll need to consider the type (external or internal frame), size, and of course price.

Both have pros and cons, but the internal frame packs are the industry favorite because they're more comfortable, easier to maneuver with, and have a greater carrying capacity. But, they are more expensive. As always, size does matter, especially here. Pack size corresponds to the amount of time on the trail—ergo, the smaller the pack, the shorter the backpacking trip. And, like everything, backpacks vary in price (anywhere from $99-$600), depending on the type and size you choose.

I like the *Osprey Ariel 65* internal pack because they designed it to fit a woman's frame, and it comes in four sizes. It's also lightweight, spacious, and has great organization features. Amazon customers give it a perfect 5.0 rating, and it sells for $290-$440 (depending on the size). Then again, if you don't want to take out a second mortgage in order to afford a backpack, take a look at the *Deuter ACT Lite 60 Women's* pack. Although it only comes in one size, it's lightweight, supportive, comfortable, and relatively inexpensive. Amazon customers give it a 4.4 rating, and it sells for $200.

Want to break away from the pack and forge your own trail? Then check out *Kelty's Trekker 65 External Frame Pack,* which is easy to load, easy to adjust, comfortable, and, of course, lightweight. Campmor customers give it a 4.6 rating, and it sells for $160.

Bear Bell

Listen up ladies, bears don't wake up in the morning, thinking, "Hey, I'm gonna go and find me some humans to harass." That's just not how it works. Truth is they only attack when they're surprised or cornered, so if you tie a bell to your pack, the bear will know you're coming and beat feet. I like *Coghlan's Bear Bell with Magnetic Silencer*. Amazon customers give it a 4.5 rating, and it sells for $6.

Bear-Resistant Food Container

A few states mandate that backpackers carry a bear-resistant food container, and although some people resist them because they're bulky and heavy, most conform to the law in order to avoid a hefty fine. So if you're hiking or backpacking in bear country, check out REI's *Bear Vault BV500 Food Container*, which gets a 4.0 rating and sells for $80. It'll keep your food safe from Yogi and other critters, but store it at least 100 yards downwind from your campsite, and never in your tent.

Bear Spray

Look, if you've tied a bell to your backpack, you shouldn't need spray, but it certainly couldn't hurt. On August 15, 2013, The Chicago Tribune reported two grizzly bear attacks in and around Yellowstone National Park, stating that bear spray was a key deterrent in one of the attacks. *Counter Assault Bear Deterrent* sells a 10.2 oz. can that also comes with a holster, so check it out. (The holster is important since I seriously doubt a bear will wait to attack until after you've pulled the spray out of your backpack.) Amazon customers give it a 4.5 rating, and it sells for $41.

Cathole Trowel

As discussed in Chapter 1, you're going to need a trowel to bury waste, and *GSI's Outdoor Cathole Trowel* is ideal for this task. It's lightweight, serrated for effortless digging, and has a sure grip for easy handling. REI and Campmor sell it for $5, and both give it a 4.7 rating. Then again, if you don't have one (or forget to pack it), a sharp stick or rock will work in a pinch.

Chair

I'll be frank. Most backpackers would rather rest against a large boulder or tree before carrying a chair in their pack, but I stumbled upon one that's so cool, I have to tell you about it. The *Alite Designs Mantis Chair* is lightweight, comfortable, durable, and portable, making it ideal for backpackers. It sits close to the ground, opens up at an angle for lounging and packs up tight in the included stuff sack. Amazon customers give it a 4.7 rating, and it sells for $90.

Coffee Maker (Drip)

I don't know about you, but I cannot start my day without coffee. Especially when I'm camping. I wish I could drink the instant kind because, well, it would be a lot easier, but I can't stand the stuff. So, if you're like me, take a look at the *GSI Outdoors Collapsible Java Drip.* It's great for backpacking because it's small, portable, lightweight, and brews directly into a coffee mug. Amazon customers give it a 4.8 rating, and it sells for $13.

Emergency Gear

If you think your cell phone will get you out of an emergency, think again. Coverage is too unreliable, meaning maybe you'll get through—maybe you won't. But, if you do need to call for help, and all you have is your cell phone as a means of communication, be smart about it. Try calling 911 first, but if you can't get through, take measures to conserve your battery. You can accomplish this by sending out a SOS text to a few of your contacts so that they can call for help. The reason? Texting uses less power than voice connect. Let them know that you're shutting off your phone to conserve the battery but that you'll power back on at a specific time in case emergency crews need to call.

Cell phone aside, did you know there are emergency call devices out there for, well, *out there*? Yep, several in fact, but I like the *SPOT-3 Satellite GPS Messenger* and the *FAST FIND 220 PLB*.

The *SPOT-3 Satellite GPS Messenger* facilitates communication using advanced satellite technology almost anywhere on the globe by sending out updates with live tracking to social media, or to a predetermined list of contacts. And if mayhem ensues, the convenient SOS button will call the nearest Search and Rescue unit for help, which I don't know, might come in handy if you get lost in the woods. It's also small, lightweight, and waterproof. Amazon customers give it a 3.9 rating, and it sells for $130. (But you're going to need an annual subscription service to power this device, and fees start at $150.)

The *Fast FIND 220 PLB* (personal locator beacon) works pretty much the same way; though, it doesn't have all the bells and whistles. Translation: it calls for help, and that's it. But, this PLB is more affordable because it doesn't require a subscription service. Amazon customers give it a 4.7 rating, and it sells for $225.

A *satellite phone* is another option, albeit an expensive one at an average cost of $800. But the goods news is, *Satmodo.com* and *SPDirect.com* will rent to you for as little as $9 per day.

A multipurpose device that could come in handy during bad weather is the rugged *Eton Scorpion Radio*. This small wonder has a digital AM/FM tuner and NOAA weather band (transmitters broadcast on frequencies that are inaudible on standard radios), which guarantees weather updates. It also has a built-in LED flashlight, USB cell phone charger, digital clock and headphone jack, powered by its built-in solar panel or hand crank. Amazon customers give it a 4.0 rating, and it sells for $60.

Another piece of emergency gear worth consideration is the *SOL Origin Essential Tool Survival Kit*. SOL stands for "survive outdoors longer," and you will with this kit. Its compact design fits in the palm of your hand, and it's light, efficient, durable, and waterproof. It's loaded with helpful items, including small fish hooks and lines, safety pins, a sewing needle, fire starter and tinder. But wait, there's more. This little kit also has a button compass, signal mirror, a knife, whistle, LED light, 3 square feet of aluminum foil, and 6 feet of stainless steel safety wire. Which is impressive enough, but it also has survival instructions with 62 lifesaving tips and techniques. Talk about small, but mighty. Amazon customers give it a 4.2 rating, and it sells for $32.

Fire Starters

I know those waterproof matches might seem like a good idea, but they're not. Trust me, just skip them and buy a decent lighter. You're going to need one of these babies no matter how you choose to camp, so you might as well get a good one. *Zippo's Brushed Chrome Lighter* is a classic, affordable at $17, and Campmor customers give it a perfect 5.0 score. This little guy requires lighter fluid though, so remember to fill it up *before* your trip; otherwise, you'll end up cold and hungry.

On the other hand, if you want to truly "get your Tarzan on," take a look at this no fuel-required option. The *UCO Light My Fire Mini Swedish Firesteel* creates an incredibly hot spark, for easy fire building in all types of weather. It's durable, works even when wet, and is International Survival Instructors Association approved. Campmor customers give it a 4.7 rating, and it sells for $8.

First Aid Kit

Okay backpackers, you're going to need a first aid kit because, well, backpacking can be dangerous. I like the *Adventure Medical Kits Ultralight/Watertight .7 First Aid Kit* because it's lightweight, but has all the essentials. Campmor customers give it a 4.5 rating, and it sells for $23. (Which, in my humble opinion, is worth it.)

Ground cloths

Don't forget a ground cloth for underneath your tent to keep it dry, and to save the floor from punctures and abrasions. A Mylar space blanket or a Tyvek ground cloth will usually do the trick, but if you want something a little more substantial, then check out Campmor's *8' X 10' Ultralight Backpacking Tarp*. Weighing in 50% lighter than most, it's also very durable, extremely water-resistant, and comes in two other sizes. And while we're on the subject, it stands to reason that tent size dictates ground cloth size, so it shouldn't extend too far beyond your tent. But if it does, tuck the edges under so that condensation doesn't collect underneath the tent floor. Campmor customers give it a 4.4 rating, and it sells for $90.

Hammock

If you're comfortable sleeping suspended between two trees, and would prefer to skip the tent, tarp, and sleeping pad altogether, take a look at *Lawson's Blue Ridge Camping Hammock*. It offers shelter like a tent, is lightweight, easy to set up, and most importantly—bug and weather resistant. And no worries if you can't find two appropriately spaced trees because it also functions like a traditional ground tent. Amazon customers give it a 4.3 rating, and it sells for $170. All that said, if you just need one for lounging, see hammocks under **Gear for Car/RV Camping.**

Knife

Listen up backpackers, I'm not talking about butter knives here. I'm referring to the type of knife that you could gut a deer or open a tin can with; this knife is so sharp. Let's face it, you need to be prepared for anything when you're camping in the backwoods, which is why you should consider the all-purpose

Gerber Big Rock Fixed Blade Knife. Amazon customers give it a 4.8 rating, and it sells for $30.

The *Victorinox Swiss Army Camper Knife* will cut stuff and then some. This little wonder is only 1" wide and 3.5" long, but it has two blades, a corkscrew, a can opener, a cap lifter, wire stripper and a key ring. But I'm not done; it also has a screwdriver, tweezers, toothpick and wood saw. Campmor customers give it a 4.8 rating, and it sells for $25.

Light Sources

Although *seriously* dorky, headlamps (you know, the type miners wear) are a good lightweight, hands-free lighting option when the sun goes down. I like *Black Diamond's Spot Headlamp* because it's super bright and has multiple, customizable settings. Amazon customers give it a 4.6 rating, and it sells for $30.

You might also consider a tripod light because they're bright and can attach to almost anything. We like the *Joby Gorillatorch Adjustable & Flexible Tripod Flashlight* because of its positioning ability. Amazon customers give it a 4.6 rating, and it sells for $26.

Another light source great for backpacking is the *Black Diamond Apollo lantern* because it's LED, collapsible, lightweight, super bright, and has adjustable legs for uneven surfaces. Campmor customers give it a 4.7 rating, and it sells for $45.

Map/Navigation Devices

If your man is like most, he won't ask for directions, so you'd better take a map *and* compass (or GPS)—especially if you're backpacking in the middle of nowhere. I like *Coghlan's Lensatic*

Compass because it's compact, accurate, and simple to use. Campmor customers give it a 4.5 rating, and it sells for $8. An actual GPS will cost a lot more but may be worth it, so take a look at the *Garmin Oregon 600*. It has the best touch screen and interface of any GPS tested; fast map draws, and programmable buttons. REI customers give it a 3.9 rating, and it sells for $400.

Mess Kit

Spam doesn't appeal to you? Then you're going to need a mess kit to cook your meals. *GSI's Outdoors Extreme Mess Kit* is an excellent option because it's small, lightweight, durable and efficient. It includes a dual use non–stick frying pan, and one-quart pot, six-inch plastic bowl, a 12-fl oz. plastic cup, and a handy sack to store it in. The bowl and cup fit inside the pot and the frying pan doubles as a lid. Campmor customers give it a 4.4 rating, and it sells for $35. (You're also going to need *GSI's Outdoors Tekk Cutlery Set*, which gets the same rating, and sells for $3.)

Pillow

Although some backpackers opt to leave the pillow home in lieu of a rolled up shirt or jacket, it doesn't mean *you* have to. Check out *Thermarest's Down Pillow*. It's compact, lightweight, and the 650 goose down fill can be adjusted by adding a clothing item to the interior pocket. It comes in three sizes, two colors, gets a Campmor rating of 4.2, and sells for $30–$50.

Rope

You're going to need something to hoist your food if you're venturing into bear country, so check out *Bush Smarts Bear Star*. This nifty little system resembles a star with rope wrapped around it. The titanium line thrower is weighted, allowing for precise positioning, and quickly secures to an anchor tree. The line clip makes it easy to attach the bear-resistant food container, and the reflective rope can hold up to 250 pounds. But you won't find the *Bear Star* at Amazon, Campmor, or REI, so if you're interested, go to their website (*bushsmarts.com*). But I have to warn you, it's not cheap. This little wonder will set you back $85.

Sink

Some backpackers take along a collapsible sink for cleanup. I like the *Seattle Sports Jumbo Camp Sink* because it's durable, it holds six gallons of water, and it packs well. Campmor customers give it a 4.6 rating, and it sells for $19.

Sleeping Bags

If you're backpacking with someone you think you'll want to cuddle with at the end of the day, then check out the highly rated two-person *Feathered Friends Penguin Nano 20* sleeping bag. The folks who reviewed it claim it's the most comfortable down bag ever tested—which is quite an endorsement. It's not the lightest or cheapest sleeping bag on the market; nevertheless, the price doesn't seem so bad when you consider the fact that you'll only need one. It sells for $459, and you'll find it online at *feathredfriends.com*.

But if you'd prefer to have a sleeping bag all to yourself, then the *Mountain Hardwear UltraLamina 32* is an excellent option. This synthetic bag comes in two sizes, is lightweight, soft, compressible, warm, and durable. Campmor customers give it a 4.4 rating, and it sells for $180.

Sleeping Pad

The *Thermarest ProLite Self Inflating Mattress* is a must for underneath that sleeping bag because it'll make your time on the ground more comfortable, and in cold weather, helps prevent hypothermia. It's lightweight, packs up tightly in the accompanying stuff sack, comes in five sizes, and is an excellent all-around camping pad. Campmor customers give it a 4.9 rating, and it sells for $55-$90.

Solar Shower

You might want to consider packing a solar shower if there's a fresh water source along the trail. This nifty little invention is just a durable bag with a hook and nozzle, but just because it's simple doesn't mean it's ineffective. They make them in different sizes, but I like the five-gallon because, well, I use lots of water when I shower. The *Seattle Sports Solar Camp Shower* is a gravity style shower, so you'll need something to hang it up on when it's time to use it. Campmor customers give it a 4.6 rating, and it sells for $15.

Stove

The *Jetboil Flash Personal Cooking System* is the perfect stove for backpackers because it's compact, light, stable, has a super-fast boil time and an insulated pot. Campmor customers it a 4.9 rating, and it sells for $99.

Tents

You're going to need a durable, lightweight, weatherproof, easy to set up tent for that backpacking trip, so take a look at the *Tarptent Double Rainbow*. This high performance, three-season tent has two doors, only weighs 2 lbs., 10 oz., is capable of withstanding strong winds, and sets up in minutes. It sells for $289 and is available at *tarptent.com*.

Some backpackers opt to use a tarp for shelter in lieu of a tent, so in this case my editor recommends the *Black Diamond Mega Light*. This roomy four-person tarp shelter is bottomless, durable, lightweight, and packs up nice and tight. Amazon customers give it a 4.5 rating, and it sells for $217.

Walking (aka trekking) Poles

I discuss the benefits of walking poles in Chapter 7, but for now, just know that you're probably going to need them if you're planning to backpack or go on a strenuous day hike. I like the *Black Diamond Trail Trekking Poles-Women* because they're made specifically for us; they pack small, are easy to adjust on the go, have adjustable straps, and are sturdy. In short, they are a good "all around" pole with an excellent balance of comfort, features, and affordability. Amazon customers give them a 4.9 rating, and they sell for $90.

Water Filters

The "granddaddy" of all portable water filters is the *Katadyn Pocket Water Filter*. It is the most rugged, highest quality, and longest lasting water filter on the market. But it'll cost you—Amazon customers give it a 4.7 rating, and it sells for a whopping $300.

If you're looking for something more affordable, check out the *MSR AutoFlow Gravity Filter*. This alternative combines water filtration, collection, and storage, into a single lightweight system. It's compact, easy to use, quick, and efficient. Amazon customers give it a 4.8 rating, and it sells for $99.

Still, if you want something even *more* affordable, check out the *Sawyer Squeeze Water Filter*. It only weighs three ounces and is simple to use. Just fill it up, squeeze and drink; there's no pumping necessary. REI customers give it a 4.5 rating, and it sells for $40.

Some backpackers skip water filters altogether, opting instead for iodine tablets such as *Potable Aqua*. Although these tablets are a lightweight, affordable option, they are not effective against Cryptosporidium (a hardy microscopic bug). But they are good at killing the smaller bugs (i.e., bacteria, viruses, and Giardia). So if this is a concern, you could use a relatively inexpensive water filter to remove the larger critters, and then use iodine tablets to kill the smaller critters. Portable Aqua sells for $7, and you can pick some up at Walmart, or order it from Amazon, Campmor or REI.

Wine Glasses, etc.

I'd skip the wine glasses when backpacking Diva, but do take the *Platypus PlatyPreserve Wine Preservation System*. It's a BPA-free, collapsible plastic container that offers a secure, lightweight alternative to packing wine. It's ideal for backpackers, and the airtight design keeps it fresh by minimizing oxygen exposure. Amazon customers give it a 4.7 rating, and it sells for $10.

GEAR FOR CAR/RV CAMPERS
Air Mattress or Cot

Unless you enjoy sleeping on the hard ground, you're going to need an air mattress or cot. There are plenty to choose from, but I like *Coleman's 4-in-1 Quickbed Twin/King Air Bed* because it's comfortable, durable, *and* versatile. Either fold the two twin beds together (don't worry, it has hinges) to create an elevated bed or zip up the two for a king sized slumber. Campmor customers give it a 4.6 rating, and it sells for $60. And to save your breath, you're going to need something to blow it up with, so don't forget the pump. *Coghlan's 4D Battery Quick Pump* works great, and it's affordable. Amazon customers give it a 4.0 rating, and it sells for $12.

I'm not comfortable sleeping on a cot, but if you are, take a look at *REI's Camp Folding Cot*. It has a sturdy aluminum frame and legs, holds up to 300 lbs., and folds in half for easy transport and storage. It gets a 4.2 rating and sells for $80.

BBQ Grills

Although my Tarzan likes to swing from the trees, he doesn't have much patience for charcoal, which is why we own *Weber's*

Q1000 Portable Propane Gas Grill. It's portable, has a handy push-button ignition for easy start up, a temperature control valve, and a removable catch pan for easy clean-up. Amazon customers give it a 4.7 rating, and it sells for $170.

On the other hand, if you're on a budget and you have all the time in the world to BBQ, take a look at *Weber's Smokey Joe Grill.* This little guy is also portable, easy to clean, cooks great, and is much more affordable. Amazon customers give it a 4.7 rating, and it sells for $30.

Bear Accessories

Please refer back to **Gear for Backpackers** if you're planning to pitch a tent, or hike in bear country, because odds are, you're going to need bear spray or a bell.

Chairs

There are a lot of camp chairs to choose from, but beware; they're not all created equally. And don't pass on this item, thinking you can get by with your beach chair because you can't. They sit close to the ground and trust me on this; you do not want to be nose to nose with the metal fire ring. I like *Coleman's Oversized Quad Chair with Cooler* because it's sturdy, has adjustable armrests, a cup holder, side storage, and, of course—a little cooler. Amazon customers give it a 4.5 rating, and it sells for $30.

Coffee Makers

The European method of pressing coffee is great for camping, especially if you're impatient and can't wait 15 minutes for your morning cup of Joe. If this applies to you, check out the *Thermos Vacuum Insulated Stainless-Steel Gourmet Coffee Press.* It makes great coffee and is convenient and efficient. Just add boiling water, wait 4 minutes, then press. Campmor customers give it a 4.6 rating, and it sells for $38.

If you're brewing coffee for a crowd (and you have the space to store it), you might want to consider *Coleman's Portable Propane Coffee Maker with Stainless Steel Carafe.* It brews 10 cups in 15 minutes, is durable, requires no cords or stove, and is powered by a propane cylinder. Amazon customers give it 4.5 rating, and it sells for $84.

The good old-fashioned percolator is also an excellent option for camping and will appeal to all you traditionalists out there. Take a look at the *GSI Outdoors Glacier Stainless Percolator,* which is rigid, built to last, and easy to use. Campmor customers give it a 4.7 rating, and it sells for $25–$50, depending on the size.

Cooler

A cooler is a staple for car campers and also comes in handy when RV camping. Although we manage to cram a whole lot of food in our trailer's little refrigerator, there's never enough room for beverages. Seriously, the bottled water, orange juice, half and half, milk, soda, beer, wine, and—sometimes—vodka just won't fit. I like *Coleman's 54 Quart Steel-Belted Cooler.* It's durable, easy to carry, and keeps our drinks nice and cold. And while we're on the subject, don't splurge for the wheels. They might *seem* like a great idea at the store, but not so much when you're bumping your way over the rocks, logs, dirt, or sand. Amazon customers give it a 4.3 rating, and it sells for $110.

Daypacks

You're going to need a daypack if you're planning to venture away from your campsite, so take a look at the *Deuter Speed Lite 20*. This pack is lightweight, equipped with a Velcro tab for the hydration hose, and has innovative buckles for side storage. Amazon customers give it a 4.7 rating, and it sells for $89. But if you don't want to spend that much money on a daypack, *REI's Flash 18* is half the price, but still a decent option.

Dishes

You have a few choices here. Either buy the disposable variety (paper or plastic) or stock up on reusable "camp friendly" dishes. I'm no tree hugger, but I love trees, so I'm not fond of paper plates. But at least they're biodegradable and won't linger in our landfills for 100 years. And let's be honest; they're convenient. So I guess it comes down to preferences. What's worse: Wasting trees, filling up our landfills with plastic, or wasting precious water? I'll let you decide. Me? I like to use my acrylic dishes purchased from the Dollar Store if I have access to plenty of water. If not, I use sturdy paper plates.

However, if you'd rather have something a little more permanent, then check out *Coleman's 24-piece Speckled Enamelware & Cutlery Set*. It's a set of four that comes with 10-inch plates, 10-oz mugs, six-inch bowls, knives, spoons, and forks. Although it gets mixed reviews, it's practical, and the cutlery comes with a cool little carrying case that wraps up tightly. Amazon customers give it a 3.7, and it sells for $41.

Dustpan/Broom

A small broom (i.e., whisk) and dustpan are a necessity around the campsite. I use mine all the time to sweep tents, picnic tables, chairs, rugs, our trailer floor, my husband—you name it. Which reminds me. Don't forget a doormat for your RV because it will substantially reduce your sweeping time. You can find an inexpensive broom set and doormat at Home Depot, Target or Walmart.

Emergency Gear

Campers who plan to tackle a strenuous day hike should consider the *Emergency Zone Deluxe Survival Bottle Kit*. It's lightweight, compact, and everything fits into the one-liter waterproof bottle. This emergency kit includes Band-Aids and antiseptic wipes, etc., but the emergency blanket, poncho, whistle, multi-tool pliers, and LED flashlight make it especially useful. Amazon customers give it a 4.3 rating, and it sells for $27.

Fire Starter

Another little item that you can't live without is a long-necked lighter for those hard to reach places (like your trailer's pilot light in the back of the oven). *Bic* makes them for around $3 each, and you can pick one up at the same place you buy your dustpan, broom, and doormat.

First Aid Kit

The *Adventure Medical Kits, Family First Aid,* is an excellent all-purpose kit for the campsite. It contains a medical guide, essential equipment, wound management items, blister items, bandage materials, and medications such as antihistamine and ibuprofen. Campmor customers give this kit a perfect 5.0 rating, and it sells for $25.

Games

If you're planning to camp with children or a group, you're going to need some board games or a group activity to keep your campers, uh...well, happy. I discuss games in greater detail in Chapter 6, but for now just know that I've listed them under gear because when you're camping with children, games are almost as important as your sleeping bag.

Generator

These nifty machines will save the day during a power outage *and* your camping trip. But watch out, they're not all created equally. Long story short, camping generators should be quiet, lightweight, and fuel-efficient. For these reasons, the Honda and Yamaha generators are best for camping. But they're not cheap. Our *Yamaha EF2400IS* cost $1,200 a few years ago but sells for $1,400 today.

So, if you're planning to camp more than once a year, you should seriously consider buying or renting a generator. (Rentals cost around $30 per day.) Our trailer runs mostly on its battery, but if we want to microwave popcorn, use a blow dryer, run the air conditioning or power our movie projector, we have to turn on the generator. Which reminds me, although it's quieter than most, you can still hear it, so we use it sparingly. In other words, we don't leave it on for extended periods of time. And when we watch a movie, we carry it 100 feet into the woods so that it doesn't drown out said movie.

Ground Cloths

You car campers are going to need something underneath that tent to prevent condensation and abrasions. I discussed ground cloths in **Gear for Backpackers,** so if you need a refresher (or if you skipped that section altogether), please go back.

Hammock

Ahhh…the hammock. In my opinion, there's nothing better than stretching out in one after a long hike, or a short one for that matter. The key, of course, is finding two perfectly spaced trees. I like the *Bliss Single Hammock* because it's compact, lightweight, made out of super durable nylon parachute silk and features a side storage pocket. It's also wide (4'7") and long (9'8"), and it holds up to 350 lbs. Amazon customers give it a 4.8 rating, and it sells for $45. But if you get one, you'll also need a knot-tying app, or at the very least, a knot-tying lesson. The *Knot Guide* is a good app for iPhone users and sells for $1.99. Android users should take a look at the *How to Tie Knots* app, which is free.

Knife

Car and RV campers are probably going to need a sharp knife to fight off the critters. Just kidding! I covered this under **Gear**

for Backpackers, so please go back because odds are, you're going to need one.

Light Sources

You're going to need something to light up your campsite after the sun goes down, so don't forget the flashlight and lantern.

If you don't already own a flashlight, skip the traditional type and purchase a new LED flashlight instead. LED stands for *light emitting diode* (whatever that means). What I do know is this: LED flashlights work just as well and are just as reliable, however, they last longer. (Meaning they're better for the environment because they use fewer batteries.) So if all of this makes sense to you, take a look at the *Princeton Tec Impact XL Led Flashlight.* This little wonder is bright, durable, has a long battery life, and is waterproof. Campmor customers give it a 4.8 rating, and it sells for $30.

The good old-fashioned lantern is my preferred light source because you can hang it up, or stand it upright on a flat surface. And there are several types to choose from, such as butane, propane, candle, solar, or LED. I like the *Rayovac Sportsman* because it's sturdy, compact, super bright, and LED powered. Amazon customers give it a 4.6 rating, and it sells for $25. But another lantern that deserves a shout out is the revolutionary *MPOWERED Luci Solar Lantern.* This little guy is inflatable, packable, lightweight, rechargeable, waterproof, and 80 lumens bright. Eight hours in the sun will generate 6–12 hours of light, and it also has a flashing light setting for emergency situations. The only drawback that could be a problem for some campers is the limited light radius (15 square feet). Amazon customers give it a 4.5 rating, and it sells for $15.

Mallet

A sturdy rubber mallet is a helpful tool for setting up your tent, badminton or volleyball net, so check out *Coghlan's Rubber Tent Peg Mallet*. The head hammers the metal or plastic stakes into the ground, and the hook grabs hold, for easy removal. Amazon customers give it a 3.8 rating, and it sells for $5.

Navigation Devices

Stop! Navigate back to **Gear for Backpackers** if you think you'll be venturing away from your campsite for a day hike or a little exploring.

Rope

Although some of you will wish you had a rope to strangle your neighbor with, that's not why I'm recommending it. Backpackers use it for various reasons, mostly to elevate their food so that bears can't get to it, but it's also handy around the campsite. Consider purchasing some durable *Paracord*, which is a commercial grade parachute cord. Fifty feet should be long enough, and you can pick some up at REI, Target, or Walmart for around $5.

Shade Canopy

Unless you're camping in the redwoods, you're going to need shade for your campsite. We set up a canopy over our metal bear box whenever we're in bear country because they get *extremely hot,* especially during the summer months. We also set up one over our picnic table, or at the beach or lake when we're camping with friends. I like *Coleman's Instant Wide Base Canopy* because it's easy to transport, easy to set up, and easy to store. It measures 12' X 12' when open and provides 81 square feet of shade. Amazon customers give it a 3.9 rating, and it sells for $109.

Sink

Washing dishes can be a little tricky if you don't have a sink, so check out *Prepworks from Progressive International's Collapsible Dish Tub.* The main difference between this and the backpacking tub is the rigid design. Ladies, I came across some pretty elaborate sinks and washing stations while researching this subject, but save your money; this is no time to splurge. Your little collapsible dish tub will accomplish the same thing. Amazon customers give it a 4.9 rating, and it sells for $17.

Sleeping Bags

Because weight isn't an issue for car or RV campers, you might want to take a look at the *Wenzel Grande.* This bag is considered by many to be the best "cold weather car camping bag," and it's fairly reasonable at $79. Then again, *Wenzel's Conquest* wins the best value award at $55. Both are available on Amazon and scored a 4.7 rating. But if you're willing to spend more, take a look at the *Slumberjack Country Squire 20.* This bag is impressively roomy and warm, has a removable cotton sheet, a sturdy zipper, and non-skid shell fabric. Amazon customers give it a 4.2 rating, and it sells for $210.

I stumbled upon something during my research that I didn't even know existed, and because it's so cool, I'm going to share it with you. Selk makes a sleeping bag that you can actually *wear*. The official name is the *Selk'bag Original 4G*, and they market it as a sleepwear system. The fact that you can sleep in this suit is cool in and of itself, but you can also wear it outside, which makes it perfect for camping. I don't own one yet, but I plan to. They come in three sizes, six colors and have a 35 degrees Fahrenheit rating. Amazon customers give them a 4.9 rating, and they sell for $159.

S'more Grill

I know roasting marshmallows over a campfire is supposed to be a camping "rite of passage," but I get frustrated making S'mores the traditional way. My marshmallow always falls off the poker thingamajig, and I don't love that the graham cracker and chocolate aren't warm when I bite into it. Well, there's a nifty little device out there you might not be aware of that roasts the entire S'more at the same time. If this concept appeals to you, check out *Coghlan's Camper's S'mores Grill*. Amazon customers give it a 4.0 rating, and it sells for $12.

Solar Shower/Shelter

Unfortunately, some campgrounds don't have showers, so you might want to consider the no gravity required *Nemo Helio Pressure Shower*, which comes with a handy foot pump. Just leave the portable tank in the sun for a few hours, and then step on the pump for 5-7 minutes of water, delivered via a seven-foot hose. REI customers give it a 4.7 rating, and it sells for $100. And, if you're shy, you'll want to take a look at the *Privacy Pop-up Shower Shelter* by Matter of Time, Inc. Amazon customers give it a 4.1 rating, and it sells for $60. But if you need something a little bigger, the *Lightspeed Outdoors Camping Shower Tent* has a built in clothesline and storage pockets. Amazon customers give it a 4.7 rating, and it sells for $125.

Stove

The powerful burners, generous cooking area, and efficient flame control make the *Camp Chef Everest* an ideal stove for car and RV campers. Also, it's wind resistant and easy to set up. Prices vary depending on where you purchase it, but I found the best deal on Amazon. It gets a 4.4 rating and sells for $110.

Tents

Yikes, there are so many tents to choose from, researching this subject made my head spin! They come in different sizes and shapes, so in the interest of time (and my sanity), here are four spacious, three-season tents worth consideration. (The number after the name indicates the amount of people the tent sleeps.)

Name	Why I Like It	Score	Price
REI Half Dome 2	Excellent Value	4.5	$189
Marmot Limelight 4	Easy Set-up	4.8	$330
Kelty Trail Ridge 6	It's Roomy	4.7	$349
Eureka Copper Canyon 8	Moveable Divider	4.8	$380

All of the tents I've listed above are for sale on Amazon, Campmor, or REI. They are all durable, rainproof, easy to set up, have large mesh panels for stargazing and a full cover "fly" for bad weather or privacy. Equally important, all four tents have plenty of storage for your things and two doors.

Trash Can/Bags

Every campsite needs a collapsible trashcan because, well, you generate a lot of trash when you camp and because they're easier to store than a traditional can. I like *Coghlan's Pop-Up Camp Trash Can*, which is a heavy-duty plastic can. Campmor customers give it a 4.4 rating, and it sells for $12. Don't forget the trash bags for inside the can; this particular one requires 33-gallon bags.

Vinyl Tablecloth

You're going to need a sturdy vinyl tablecloth for your campsite's picnic table, so take a look at *Coghlan's 0660 Picnic Combo Pack*. The vinyl surface cleans easily, making it perfect for outdoors, and the metal clamps keep it in place. Amazon customers give it a 3.9 rating, and it sells for $9.

Walking Poles & Water Filters

Walking poles and water filters are optional gear for car and RV campers; even so, if you're feeling adventurous, or just plain curious, go back to **Gear for Backpackers.**

Wine Glasses, etc.

Wine lovers who would rather not drink their wine from a Styrofoam or plastic cup should check out *GSI's Outdoors BPA-Free Nesting Wine Glasses.* They are acrylic glasses, classic in shape, but the innovative stem screws off at the midpoint, allowing for easy storage. Campmor customers give them a 4.6 rating, and they sell for $7 each. On the other hand, if a traditional wine glass seems a bit too ambitious for the campsite, then check out *GSI's Outdoors Stemless Wine Glasses.* They are also acrylic BPA-free glasses, but the stemless design delivers greater stability on uneven surfaces. Campmor customers give them a 4.8 rating, and they also sell for $7 each.

PRODUCTS

You know that expression, "When in Rome, do as the Romans do"? Well, if you're planning a trek into the wild blue yonder, you should probably consider taking along some products that won't take the blue out of the yonder.

Now if you're car or RV camping, these products aren't *as* important as they are to a backpacker. Still, you should rethink what you throw in your pack or duffle bag before you embark on *any* camping trip. And here's why: 1) If your deodorant, lotion, or soap smells good to you, it'll also smell good to critters and bears. 2) Most soaps leave a harmful residue behind, which isn't great for our streams and lakes.

Look, your time is valuable, so I'm not going to waste it by telling you which sunscreen, etc. to buy. But what I will do is discuss a few "outdoor friendly" cosmetics that you can use on the down-low, and highlight some products that might be new to you.

All-purpose biodegradable soap

Dr. Bonner's Magic Soaps, 18-in-1 Hemp Peppermint Pure-Castile Soap may be a mouthful to pronounce, but is worthy of all the words. This product is an all-natural, organic certified, biodegradable, multi-purpose wonder soap that cleans your body, your hair, your dishes, your clothes, and even your pets. And because you only need one bottle to accomplish so many things, it's perfect for backpacking and camping. The 16-oz. bottle gets a 4.6 rating on Amazon and sells for around $10.

Beauty & Hair

Okay, here's the thing. I don't wear a lot of makeup when we camp because it's just not practical. But if you're still trying to impress your man, then there are a few ways to "get your glam on" without it being obvious.

To begin with, moisturizing your face will make you look and feel better, and since you'll also need sunscreen, purchase a good **moisturizer** with SPF. I like *A Perfect World SPF 15 BB* by Origins because it's tinted, allowing me to skip the foundation altogether. It's also appropriate for all skin types. A 1.7-oz. tube will set you back $35, but when you consider the fact that you're getting a multi-purpose product, the price tag doesn't seem so bad.

Nonetheless, if you *must* wear **foundation**, invest in a good *lightweight* product. I like *Hello Flawless Oxygen WOW* by Benefit Cosmetics because it's an oil-free liquid foundation for all skin types that delivers light to medium coverage. And it has UVA *and* UVB protection. You can purchase it online or from your local beauty supply store for around $35.

Although **dry shampoos** may be new to you, they've been around *almost* as long as the caveman. The long and the short of it is they absorb excess oils and build volume, and are great for in-between shampoos. Sadly, they haven't invented any that remove dirt, but if you manage to get through your day without rolling around in your campsite, a dry shampoo should make you feel good as new. At least until your next wash, that is. If this sounds like a good idea to you, take a look at *Umberto Beverly Hills Dry Clean Dry Shampoo. TotalBeauty.com* users give it an 8.2 rating (out of 10), and it sells for $10. Another one worth consideration is *Batiste Dry Shampoo (Original).* Your mother may have used this back in the day because this company has been making in-between shampoos for over 40 years. Amazon customers give it a 4.4 rating, and it also sells for $10.

If a dry shampoo isn't your thing and you *have* to wash your hair, consider a **leave-in conditioner.** I use them frequently when we camp because they're a great compromise (i.e., way to save water). *Real Simple* magazine likes *TREsemme's Split Remedy Leave In-Condition Spray,* which sells for around $6 and is available at most drugstores.

And while you're at it, pick up some *tinted lip balm, waterproof mascara,* **a** *compact mirror,* and don't forget *hair bands* **or** *clips* if you don't like wearing hats.

Citronella Lantern, Candle, & Sticks

There's much debate among mosquito haters about the effectiveness of citronella, and I'm one of the debaters. My husband swears by it; me, not so much. Still, at the end of the day, it certainly couldn't *hurt*, so check out *Coleman's Citronella Candle Lantern*. It repels mosquitoes for up to 50 hours *and* provides ambiance. Amazon customers give it a 4.1 rating, and it sells for $11. Another good option is the *Lamplight TIKI 17-oz. Galvanized Citronella Wax Bucket*. Amazon customers give it a 3.8 rating, and it sells for $12. But if you prefer sticks, take a look at *New Mountain NM-12 Sandalwood Mosquito Sticks*. Amazon customers give them a 4.4 rating, and they sell for $16.

Insect Repellents

This is a tricky one because finding a product that truly works has been a challenge since the first caveman (or woman) poked his or her head out of the cave. While researching this subject, I stumbled upon a great article published May 25, 2010, by *Consumer Reports Health* on WebMD, and since they are a trusted source, I'm going to share their findings. After extensive human testing, Consumer Reports Health recommends the following six insect repellents:

	Product	Active Ingredient
1	*Off Deep Woods Sportsmen II*	30% Deet
2	*Cutter Backwoods Unsented*	23% Deet
3	*Off Family Care Smooth & Dry*	15% Deet
4	*3M Ultrathon Insect Repellent*	25% Deet
5	*Repel Lemon Eucalyptus*	Oil of L.E.
6	*Natrapel 8-Hour*	20% Picaridin

Now, let's talk about the active ingredient, DEET. There are folks out there who believe it's toxic when ingested into the central nervous system. Well, I'm no doctor, but if *Consumer Reports Health* deems it safe when used as directed, then I'm going to use it as directed. Still, you should avoid repellents containing more than 30% DEET, and don't apply it to your baby if he or she is younger than two months old. Personally, I wouldn't put it on my baby at all, but that's just me. Apply it sparingly and only to exposed skin, and avoid getting it in your eyes, mouth, or in cuts. Another important point worth mentioning is that you should avoid products that mix sunscreen with DEET insect repellent because sunscreens are meant to be used generously, and DEET is meant to be used sparingly. These two products contradict each other, and in my opinion, should not be in the same bottle.

All that said, if you'd rather not use DEET on your child, then check out *Simba's Baby/Kids Natural Mosquito Repellent Bracelet.* They're an excellent alternative to traditional insect repellents, come in fun neon colors, smell good, and are reusable. Amazon customers give them a 3.7 rating, and they cost $7. And, as of today, there are natural, DEET-free repellents on the market, though they get mixed reviews. Still, new ones are being developed even as I type this sentence, so if you're in mosquito country, and you're looking for a natural alternative, then by all means Google it.

I know this is a lot to process. But if you think that maybe you could put up with a few ticks or mosquitoes, just remember this: deer ticks sometimes carry Lyme disease, and mosquitoes sometimes carry the West Nile virus. That's all I'm going to say about *that*.

Insect Bite Treatments

I wish I could tell you that if you use a good repellent, you won't need a bite ointment, but I'd be lying. Sometimes the little buggers just get in. So, to be safe, toss some of *PIC's Bite Relief* into your first aid kit. The multi-action formula of anesthetic and antiseptic delivers instant pain and itch relief from mosquito, bees, wasps, hornets, ant, and spider bites or stings. It gets a 5.0 rating and sells for $4. *Tender After Bite Outdoor* also gets a perfect score and costs the same as PIC. Isn't it nice to have options?

Poison Ivy/Oak Products

You do *not* want to brush up against poison ivy, poison oak, or poison sumac. But if you do, you'll need some advice and product information, which I discuss at length in Chapter 5. So read on my friend.

Toilet Paper

I know you're thinking, "Really?" Yes, really. There's a special toilet paper for backpackers and even RV'ers. *Coghlan's Backpacking Toilet Paper* is good because not only is it soft, strong, and absorbent, but its compact packaging and biodegradability make it ideal for backpackers. It gets a 4.7 rating and sells for $4.

We buy special biodegradable toilet paper for our trailer because my husband's afraid the traditional stuff will clog our black tank. Although there's some truth to this, some traditional brands are perfectly fine. To figure out whether or not yours is RV safe, do the "jar test." Take a clear glass jar with a lid and fill it halfway with water. Then, add a few squares of your favorite TP and close the jar. Shake it up for about 10 seconds and take a look. If the tissue breaks up into little pieces, it's safe to use in your trailer, camper, or motor home. If not, try a different brand or spring for the stuff that says, "RV safe" on the label.

Wipes, Wipes, & More Wipes

Bath

These handy little bath wipes are used by nurses as well as outdoor enthusiasts and are perfect for campers. *Adventure Medical Kits Fresh Bath Wipes* come in a package of 8, gets good ratings, and sells for $5. They're not much bigger than a regular handy wipe; nevertheless, they're an excellent heavy-duty, anti-bacterial, appropriate for all body parts, no-rinse bathing solution.

Dog

Yep, they even make them for your furry friend. I'll discuss these, and other products for dogs in Chapter 6.

Facial

I like to use wet cleansing towelettes for removing my mascara (etc.) at the end of the day, and they're perfect for camping because they don't require water. But in the mornings, I like the dry facial cloths because they get nice and sudsy with a little water (which helps clear my cobwebs). The key ingredient, of course, is water, so if you're in short supply, then wet wipes are perfectly fine. Olay makes both types, and they are available at most drug stores.

Wet Ones

You know what they are, and where to buy them. But hear me when I say don't forget them! I use the stand-up plastic canister type for our campsite and the flat purse type for my beach bag and daypack.

CHAPTER 3 TIPS

- ✓ Amazon, Campmor, and REI sell most of the items discussed in this chapter; however, Target and Walmart also sell essential camping supplies and gear.

- ✓ Not sure if you want to invest in gear for an activity you might hate? Rent it first from *LowerGear.com.*

- ✓ Reflective rope will prevent stumbles in the night. So if your tent or tarp, etc. needs to be tied down, it might be wise to pick some up.

- ✓ Whole Foods and Trader Joe's have a good selection of "natural" fragrance-free products, which are great for camping.

- ✓ If you'd rather skip the DEET, try Ben Gay. Apparently bugs don't like the way it smells either.

Four

Dining Out...
Outdoors, That Is

June 13, 2014
West Shore, Lake Tahoe
Jeez. It took my large pot of water so long to boil,
our camping pals almost declared mutiny!

I love to cook, and figured out pretty quickly that I could produce the same gourmet style meals without my five-burner stove, double oven, and large granite island. It's just a little trickier; that's all. That said, it did take me a little while to perfect my current system of planning, listing, shopping, and preparation, which I'm happy to share.

Get a piece of lined paper and draw three vertical lines. List *every* meal for every day. I know this may sound tedious, but trust me, you don't want to forget the wine. I mean butter!

Listing System

Front

DAY	MENU	GROCERIES
FRI/Dinner	Tri tip roast	Marinated tri tip
	Baked potatoes	Potatoes
	Asparagus	Sour cream
SAT/Breakfast	Breakfast burritos	Green onions
	Coffee & juice	Asparagus
SAT/Lunch	Ham sandwiches	Tortillas
	Chips	Eggs
SAT/Dinner	BBQ chicken	Shredded cheese
	Corn on the cob	Ham
	Salad	Bell pepper
SUN/Breakfast	Cinnamon rolls	Salsa
	Pineapple	Half & Half
	Coffee & juice	OJ
SNACKS, etc	Apples, Salami &	Bread
	Cheese, S'mores	Lettuce
DRINKS	Soda, Hot Choc,	Chips
	Beer & Wine	Chicken
		Corn on the cob
		Cinnamon rolls
		Pineapple
		Salami
		Cheddar cheese
		Marshmallows
		Chocolate
		Hot Chocolate
		Beer

Back

PACK
Butter
Olive oil
Balsamic vinegar
S&P shakers
Milk
Coffee
Swiss cheese
Tomato
Mayo
Mustard
BBQ sauce
Salad dressing
Cucumber
Red onion
Apples
Graham crackers
Wine
Beer
Paper plates
Plastic cups
Paper towels
Hand wipes
Dish soap
Tin foil
Sandwich bags

The groceries column *will not* line up with the day and menu columns. The idea is that you make the meal list *before* the grocery list. Then, going down the meal column line-by-line, jot down what you need to buy, and on the back, what you need to pack. (So, you'll be flipping the list over and back as you go.) Mostly, the back "pack" list is for kitchen staples, beverages, and things I already have in my pantry, but sometimes I add stuff like paper plates.

Preparation

"By failing to prepare, you are preparing to fail." Ben Franklin said that. Look, cooking at home with running water and electricity is challenging enough, so why oh why would you opt to rinse, slice, and dice in your campsite? I'm embarrassed to say that it took me a little while to figure this one out; even so, I did, so listen up.

Rinse everything *before* you go. Otherwise, you'll be marching back and forth from your campsite to the community faucet (or wasting your trailer's water reserve). Which is fine, I guess if you need the exercise. But honestly, wouldn't you rather be relaxing by the campfire? I rinse *everything* ahead of time, including my lettuce for sandwiches, which I bag in a separate airtight Ziploc.

I don't go so far as to slice my tomatoes, but I do chop up most veggies like the bell pepper for our burritos and green onions for our baked potatoes. My husband likes to cook breakfast for me on our camp stove, and because I'm usually still asleep when he starts this process, I assemble a "breakfast bag" for his convenience. I put the individual ingredients into separate little "snack" bags and combine them all into one large Ziploc bag labeled "breakfast". This way, the shredded cheese, chopped bell pepper, diced ham, etc., are ready to go. (I know I'm a Diva; that's why I'm writing this book.)

Before I continue, I feel compelled to acknowledge something. My sister, Lisa, who is the polar opposite of me, was a tad annoyed by this section. So, at the risk of offending her and every "free spirit," out there, allow me to clarify. I'm not saying my way is the *only* way; I'm just saying this method works best for me. Personally, I'd rather do all the prep work at home because it's easier, but if you don't have the desire *or* the luxury of time, don't sweat it. Your meals will still come together; they'll just take a little longer that's all.

KISS (Keep it simple, Stupid!)

I always shake my head when I see car campers grilling burgers. Although it may seem like the logical thing to do (being outside and all), it isn't very efficient. For example, let's count the ingredients that you'll need to make that hamburger:

1. Ground beef
2. Seasoning
3. Buns
4. Cheese
5. Lettuce
6. Tomato
7. Onion
8. Pickle
9. Mustard

10. Mayo
11. Ketchup

Yikes, that's a lot of ingredients. You could cram all of them into your cooler, or you could opt instead for a pre-made or marinated entrée from your grocer's meat department. These no-fuss meal options are perfect for camping because they don't require additional ingredients, and they're convenient and delicious. We like to grill *"Guy's Smoke Pit Beef Tri-Tip Roast Santa Maria Recipe,"* by Guy Fieri. We're also fond of our local market's Gorgonzola stuffed chicken, and their bacon wrapped pork chops. But I have to warn you; you probably won't save any money going this route, but you *might* save your sanity.

Skillet dinners, found in your grocer's freezer, are another convenient option for camping. They come in individual disposable bags and are easy to cook. Just tear, pour, fry in a skillet, and—ta-da...dinner! Consumer Reports tested several varieties and determined that *Contessa's Sesame Chicken* is economical, tasty *and* nutritious. They also like *Birds Eye's Viola Chicken Florentine.* (And while we're on the subject, don't forget a bagged salad.)

BACKPACK COOKING
Freeze-Dried Meals

I'm going to be brutally honest. I wouldn't eat one of these meals under an ordinary circumstance; however, I bet they're pretty good after a long day on the trail. I say this because the French onion soup we consumed after our 16-mile trek to Half Dome, was the best soup I've ever had. Though, in hindsight,

I have a feeling it was just average. So with this in mind, and according to numerous sources, here are the top-rated freeze-dried meals.

1. *Coleman Max Patch Mac & Cheese*
2. *Mountain House Beef Stroganoff*
3. *Mountain House Spaghetti & Meat Sauce*
4. *Mountain House Seafood Chowder*
5. *Mountain House Chicken Ala King & Noodles*
6. *Mountain House Chili Mac*
7. *Mountain House Grilled Chicken Breast w/ Mashed Potatoes*
8. *Enertia Trail Foods Switchback Shells*
9. *Enertia Trail Foods Moosilauke Goulash*

They are reasonable (from $5 to $8), and available on Amazon, Campmor, and REI.

Spice Blends

Backpackers have to get creative when it comes to meal planning because, well, you know, they're carrying their kitchens on their backs. So to maximize flavor while keeping ingredients to a minimum, they often create and take along spice blends to season up pasta, potatoes, rice, vegetables, etc. I found these spice blends on *spicesherpa.com*, which were inspired by Mark Bittman and taken from an article in the September 2010 *Backpacker Magazine*.

Mexican Blend:

One tablespoon roasted, fresh ground cumin, two teaspoons oregano, one teaspoon chili powder, and ½ teaspoon ground coriander. This blend will add zing to your rice, beans, or macaroni and cheese.

Mediterranean Blend

Equal parts dried rosemary, thyme, parsley, and/or sage. Crumble in one or two bay leaves. Take toasted pine nuts and sprinkle them along with the spice blend on pasta and olive oil or mix it with mashed potatoes.

Asian Blend

Equal parts dried garlic and powdered ginger plus a couple of pinches of brown sugar. Take some packets of soy sauce, and toasted sesame seeds to spice up rice or noodles.

Italian Blend

Equal parts dried basil, oregano, parsley, and garlic powder. This blend will wake up your pasta and rice, and to add even more flavor, take along some toasted pine nuts and some sun-dried tomatoes.

Indian Blend

One teaspoon each ground ginger, cinnamon, and cardamom, ½ teaspoon each fresh ground clove or nutmeg. This blend is delicious on chickpeas, fresh tomatoes, pita bread, or mixed in pasta.

Bagel Spice Zesty Jalapeno

This pre-made gourmet spice blend in a bottle is also good sprinkled on almost everything. It's available at most supermarkets and sells for $6.

CAR/RV COOKING
Foil Cooking

Foil cooking makes a lot of sense when you're camping because the recipes don't require a lot of ingredients; you can place the foil packs directly on the grill, and cleanup is a cinch. (No pots or pans, just crumple, and toss!) Food Network has a great selection of recipes, and because there are too many to list, I'm going to send you there. Just go to their homepage at *foodnetwork.com* and type in "50 Things to Grill in Foil" in their search section, for recipes and directions on how to make a foil bag. It's worth the effort because some of the recipes you'll find include: jalapeno poppers, spicy chicken wings, garlic shrimp, paella, glazed pork, and even popcorn. Who knew you could do some much with aluminum foil?

Dutch Oven Cooking

Your Tarzan may turn in his vine for cowboy boots if he enjoys cooking over a campfire in a Dutch oven. This form of cooking doesn't fall under the KISS principle because it requires a little bit of work and patience, but it's fun, nevertheless. Think of it this way: it's not so bad cooking a big Thanksgiving dinner once a year, but you certainly wouldn't do that every day.

There are different types of Dutch ovens, so to be clear, I'm referring to the big, black, cast iron pots with a lid. They are great for outdoor cooking because they sit directly in, or on, coals or the campfire. You'll need a few tools to go along with the oven—mostly a good pair of heat gloves, a lid lifter, and coals.

If this type of cooking appeals to you, check out *dutchovendude. com*. This website has a plethora of information, starting with how to choose the perfect oven. It also covers maintenance and cleaning, suggests helpful cooking techniques, and shares the author's favorite recipes.

Recipes

Speaking of recipes, no cooking section would be complete without a few, so here are some of my favorites, which I've adapted for the campsite.

Korean-Style Barbecued Flank Steak

Source: Better Homes & Garden/1999 Simply Perfect Grilling Issue

¼   cup green onions, finely chopped

¼   cup soy sauce (I use a little more)

2   tablespoons brown sugar

1   tablespoon toasted sesame oil

1   tablespoon grated fresh gingerroot

2   large cloves garlic, minced

1   beef flank steak (about 1 ½ pounds)

Before you go: Whisk together the green onions, soy sauce, brown sugar, sesame oil, gingerroot, and garlic. Put the steak in a plastic bag and place it in a shallow dish. Add the marinade, seal the bag, and turn to coat. Refrigerate at least 6 hours or up to 24 hours, occasionally turning.

At the campsite: Heat the grill to medium, discard the marinade and cook the steak for 17-21 minutes for medium (turning halfway through). Carve steak *across the grain* into thin slices and serve.

Steak w/ Blue Cheese Butter Sauce
Source: Food Network/Rachel Ray

- 4 steaks (your choice)
- 1 tablespoon extra-virgin olive oil
- 1 tablespoon steak seasoning (your favorite)
- 4 tablespoons butter, softened
- ½ cup blue cheese crumbles
- 2 tablespoons chopped chives

Before you go: Mix the butter, blue cheese, and chives together; wrap it in cellophane and refrigerate.

At the campsite: One hour before you start to grill, take out the pre-made butter mixture and place it in the sun to soften. Next, preheat the grill to medium. Brush the steaks with oil, sprinkle with steak seasoning and grill to desired doneness. Add a dollop or two of the butter immediately after steaks are done, so that it melts over the steaks and serve.

Grilled Chicken Cordon Bleu
Source: Food Network/Bobby Flay (adjusted)

- 4 boneless, skinless chicken breasts pounded thin
  olive oil

salt and freshly ground pepper
½ lb Gouda or aged Swiss
2 lemons, halved
8 paper-thin slices of prosciutto
¼ lb baby arugula

<u>Before you go</u>: Pound the chicken breasts, slice your preferred cheese (if it isn't already), and put both in separate Ziploc bags.

<u>At the campsite</u>: Preheat the grill to high. Brush the chicken on both sides with oil and season with salt and pepper, to taste. Grill until slightly charred on both sides and just cooked through, about 5 minutes per side. Put a few slices of cheese on each breast, close the lid and let it melt slightly, about 40 seconds. Brush the cut side of lemons with oil and grill, cut side down until golden brown and slightly charred, about 45 seconds. Top each breast with two slices of prosciutto (close the lid again for another 40 seconds). Add some arugula, squeeze the grilled lemon on top, drizzle with olive oil and serve.

Bottle o' Beer Chicken Thighs
Source: Weber's Real Grilling by Jamie Purviance

1 bottle (12 oz) beer, preferably lager
¼ cup Dijon mustard
3 tablespoons extra virgin olive oil
6 scallions, thinly sliced (light green parts only)
2 large garlic cloves, thinly sliced
1 tablespoon Worcestershire sauce

1   teaspoon kosher salt
½   teaspoon freshly ground black pepper
¼   teaspoon Tabasco sauce
8   chicken thighs (w/ bone & skin)

<u>Before you go</u>: Make the marinade, by whisking together the first nine ingredients. Pour it into an airtight, non-spill container and refrigerate. Rinse and pat dry the chicken thighs, storing them in a large Ziploc bag, and also refrigerate.

<u>At the campsite</u>: Six or 8 hours before dinner, pour the marinade into the Ziploc bag containing the chicken thighs. Press the air out of the bag and seal tightly. Turn the bag over a few times to distribute the marinade, place it in a bowl (or whatever) and refrigerate. Before dinner, preheat the grill to medium, remove the thighs from the bag and discard the marinade. Pat dry with paper towels and grill over direct, medium heat, skin side down first. Cook until the meat next to the bone is opaque (about 20 minutes), turning every 5 minutes. Serve warm.

Grilled Salmon w/ Pistachio-Basil Butter
Source: Better Homes & Gardens/1999 Simply Perfect Grilling Issue

1   cup lightly packed fresh basil leaves
6   tablespoons pistachio nuts, lightly toasted
1   tablespoon lime juice
3   cloves garlic, cut up
7   tablespoons butter (melted)
    salt & pepper

6   6 oz skinless salmon fillets
1   tablespoon cooking oil

Before you go: Combine the basil, pistachios, lime juice, garlic and butter in a food processor bowl or blender. Process or blend till the basil and pistachios are finely chopped, stopping to stir as necessary. Transfer to a bowl; season to taste with salt and pepper. Refrigerate pistachio-basil butter in a plastic bag or container.

At the campsite: One hour before you start to grill, take out the pre-made butter sauce and place it in the sun to soften. Preheat the grill to medium; brush both sides of the salmon fillets with oil, and season with salt and pepper. Grill 4-6 minutes per ½ inch thickness, turning once halfway through. Add a dollop or two of the pistachio-butter immediately after salmon is done, so that it melts over the fillets and serve.

Spicy Barbecued Shrimp Skewers
Source: Food Network/Emeril Lagasse

¼   cup vegetable or olive oil
1   tablespoon minced garlic
1   tablespoon fresh thyme
1   tablespoon chopped cilantro leaves,
1   jalapeno, seeded and minced
1   teaspoon paprika
1   teaspoon salt
1   teaspoon light brown sugar or honey

1   teaspoon ground cumin
½   teaspoon Worcestershire sauce
½   teaspoon cayenne pepper
½   teaspoon red pepper flakes
1   lime, juiced
2   lbs large shrimp, peeled & deveined

<u>Before you go</u>: Wisk together all of the marinade ingredients in a large bowl, and then pour it into a plastic container and refrigerate. Rinse the shrimp, and also refrigerate in a large Ziploc bag.

<u>At the campsite</u>: Add the marinade to the Ziploc containing the shrimp, squeezing out any excess air and seal. Let it marinade while you preheat the grill to medium. When the grill is ready, thread the shrimp onto metal skewers. Place the shrimp skewers directly on the grill and cook for about 3 minutes on each side (or until the shrimp turn pink and are lightly charred on both sides). *Do not over cook!*

Grilled Butterflied Trout w/ Lemon-Parsley Butter
Source: Food Network/Bobby Flay

4   (1 lb) trout, head removed, scaled, gutted &
    butterflied (skin on)
    olive oil or canola oil
    salt & pepper
    lemon wedges for garnish
    parsley for garnish

Lemon-Parsley Butter

1   stick unsalted butter (room temperature)
2   teaspoons finely grated lemon zest
2   tablespoons fresh lemon juice
3   tablespoons finely chopped fresh Italian parsley
    salt & pepper

Before you go: Make the Lemon-Parsley Butter by combin-
ing the softened butter, grated lemon zest, fresh lemon juice,
Italian parsley and salt and pepper to taste. Mix well, store in a
plastic container and refrigerate. Chop up about a tablespoon
of parsley for the garnish, and also refrigerate in a small Ziploc
bag.

At the campsite: One hour before you start to grill, take out
the pre-made butter sauce, place it in the sun to soften, and preheat the grill to high. Brush both sides of the trout with oil and
season with salt and pepper. Grill, skin side down, until slightly
charred and crisp, about 2–3 minutes. Carefully turn each fish
over and continue cooking until just cooked through, (3–4 minutes longer). Remove from the grill and top each fillet with 2
tablespoons of the softened Lemon-Parsley Butter. Garnish with
the parsley and lemon wedges before serving.

Grilled Pork Tenderloin Marinated in Spicy Soy Sauce
Source: Eating Well: August/September 2006

¼   cup soy sauce
2   tablespoons sugar
1   large clove garlic, minced

1   tablespoon finely grated fresh ginger
1   cayenne chili pepper, stemmed, seeded, minced
1   tablespoon toasted sesame oil
1½ pounds pork tenderloin, trimmed of fat

<u>Before you go</u>: Whisk the soy sauce and sugar in a medium bowl until the sugar is completely dissolved. Stir in garlic, ginger, chili pepper and oil, then refrigerate in a plastic bowl. Slice the pork tenderloin into one-inch thick medallions (pieces), and also refrigerate in a large Ziploc bag.

<u>At the campsite</u>: Two hours before you're ready to grill, add the marinade to the bag of pre-sliced pork medallions, being careful to squeeze out any excess air. Once you're ready to grill, preheat it to medium, remove the pork from the marinade and discard. Grill the medallions until just cooked through, (3-5 minutes per side).

Baked Potatoes
Source: Author/Dina Wills

- russet potatoes
- butter
- kosher salt
- sour cream
- chives or green onions
- aluminum foil squares

<u>Before you go</u>: Scrub your potatoes with a vegetable brush, dry well and pack them away. Rinse and chop the chives or green onions, and put them in a small Ziploc bag.

At the campsite: A few hours before you start cooking, take out some butter and place it in the sun to soften. An hour before dinner, preheat the grill to medium and poke holes in the potatoes with a fork. Next, brush them with the butter, sprinkle generously with kosher salt and wrap them loosely in aluminum foil. Place them directly on the grill for 50-60 minutes (depending on the size). Carefully peel away the aluminum foil, slice and add a couple pats of butter, a dollop of sour cream and finish with chives or green onions.

Zesty Horseradish Corn on the Cob
Source: Land O Lakes Treasury of Country Recipes

- ½   cup butter, softened
- ½   teaspoon salt
- ¼   teaspoon pepper
- 1   tablespoon chopped fresh parsley
- 2   tablespoons country-style Dijon mustard
- 2   teaspoons prepared horseradish
- 6   fresh ears of corn on the cob, husked
- 6   aluminum foil squares

Before you go: Combine all of the ingredients except for the corn in a bowl and mix well. Store in a plastic bag or container and refrigerate. Husk, rinse, and dry the corn on the cob, and also refrigerate.

At the campsite: About an hour before you start cooking, take out your butter sauce and place it in the sun to soften. While your grill is preheating, generously brush the corn with the butter and wrap it in the foil. Place it directly on the grill or over the coals or low flame, turning every 5 minutes, for 20–25 minutes.

Grilled Asparagus
Source: Author/Dina Wills

1   bunch asparagus
1   tablespoon extra virgin olive oil
1   teaspoon balsamic vinegar
    fresh ground pepper to taste

Before you go: Wash, trim, and dry the asparagus, and then refrigerate it in a Ziploc bag. Measure the extra virgin olive oil and vinegar into a plastic container and seal.

At the campsite: Preheat the grill to 350 and wipe it off. Put the asparagus on a paper plate and pour the oil and vinegar over the asparagus. Roll it around to coat and season with fresh ground pepper. Using tongs, place the asparagus directly on the grill, turning every minute or so until done (about 10 minutes).

CHAPTER 4 TIPS

- ✓ Costco has a good selection of pre-made, marinated entrees, which are perfect for camping, especially with a group.

- ✓ Backpackers, an approved TSA travel bottle kit is an excellent way to transport your cooking oil and spices.

- ✓ If you can't find metal skewers, soak wooden skewers in water for 10 minutes, so they don't catch fire. They're cheaper and work just as well.

- ✓ Allow extra time to boil water if you're cooking at a high altitude. (For more information on this subject, see Additional Reading at the back of this book.)

- ✓ Starbucks makes a respectable instant coffee if you'd prefer to skip the drip, percolator, or press.

Five

The Wild Things,
& Where They Are

June 21, 2010
<u>West Shore, Lake Tahoe</u>

Oh Lord. Tonight our friend "drunk George" told a ranger that the bear who visited our campsite was a female bear. Ranger: "Well sir, that's difficult to determine—even for us." George: "I know it was a female bear...I could tell by the way she was walking!"

There's something about being outdoors that makes you want to commune with the animals that live, well, outdoors. After all, Bambi is so cute! And Alvin and the Chipmunks have that adorable Christmas song, for crying out loud. I hate to spoil your fun, but chipmunks, squirrels, and deer have parasites, and those parasites sometimes carry disease. And, while I'm on the subject, you should know that although cute, blue jays, geese, and raccoons are downright mean. Seriously, the jays will dive bomb you for food, a goose will chase you for it, and trust me, you don't want to get into a scuffle with a raccoon. They have very long, very sharp claws and can be vicious.

Before I started camping, I'd experienced the wrath of a blue jay and a few geese, but only recently faced the wrath of a raccoon. We tried to shoo one away from our campsite, and the dang thing stood up on his hind legs, hissed, and swiped at us. Then he started throwing stuff. Well, I'm exaggerating a little, but this raccoon had a really bad attitude.

Critter Free Campsites

Your health, sanity, and wallet could be affected if you don't store your food properly. (A bold statement, I know, but allow me to explain.)

Those parasite-infested animals that I mentioned in paragraph one have ticks, which sometimes carry illness such as Rocky Mountain spotted fever and Lyme disease. Also, stay away from mice and rat droppings, because the Hantavirus, which can be fatal in humans, is spread through their urine and feces. And then there's rabies…but I'm getting ahead of myself.

And it'll make you crazy when critters help themselves to your food because, unless there's a store nearby, someone's going without soda, chips, or a sandwich. I've witnessed critters feasting like guests at a picnic table more times than I can count. Sometimes the human occupants are nowhere to be seen; other times they're there but have their backs turned.

Additionally, leaving food out can also be expensive, as there are laws against it. The fines enacted to enforce these laws vary from state to state; however, in California the fine is $1,000. And although this may seem harsh, you should know that they didn't create this law to ruin your camping trip—it exists to save the bears, (etc.).

Bear Boxes, etc.

A critter free campsite is accomplished by exercising proper food storage etiquette. In other words, unless being consumed or prepared for consumption, all food, beverages, and toiletries must be stored in a bear box or vehicle. Just last summer, we watched a very annoyed ranger cite a rowdy group of twenty-somethings whose campsite looked like a scene out of *Animal House*. (Apparently, his warning from the day before hadn't registered.) So the moral of the story is this: unless you don't mind parting with one thousand dollars, you'd better keep your food locked up nice and tight.

If you're not in bear country, and there are no bear boxes, then you should store your groceries and cooler, etc., in your car. (Covered and out of sight, with your windows up, of course.) And never store food, beverages or toiletries in your tent! Out of sight doesn't mean out of mind for critters because they can smell your goodies from a mile away.

Now, if you're paying attention, you should be thinking, "Hey, wait a minute! Didn't a bear invade her truck?" And the answer is yes, which is why I feel qualified to elaborate on this subject. We forgot to roll up the windows the night that bear helped himself to our potato chips. (I'll blame it on the moon, which was full. In fact, it was so light out when we pulled into the campground that night, we decided to take a short walk to the water before setting up. I'll never forget the moonbeam that reached out to us from across the lake. It was dreamy. However, as we were admiring this scene, a very agile, very smelly bear was wiggling into the passenger side of our truck, pulling down the weather stripping in the process. When we went back to set up camp, the bear jumped out and ran frog-like right past my husband. It was cute, but again, the stench it left behind was not pleasant.)

So because we've had our share of critter encounters, we're vigilant about food storage and throwing away our trash. We never leave either out (not even for a minute), and we take our trash to the dumpsters after every meal.

Critters & Rabies

A few paragraphs back I told you the story about the **raccoon** with attitude, but I left out the fact that they are **the most common carrier of rabies.** That's another reason to steer clear of them. Rabies is a fatal viral disease of dogs and other mammals, causing madness and convulsions. It spreads via saliva (bites) and if untreated, is nearly always fatal in humans. Other critters on the "most likely to carry rabies" list include **foxes, bats, skunks,** and **coyotes.** Sometimes badgers, weasels, wolves, mountain lions, and other mammals contract the disease, but these cases are pretty rare.

Wild animals with an advanced case of rabies may appear restless or aggressive, don't fear humans, snap at the air or turn in circles, drool a lot, and can be partially or fully paralyzed. If you witness, any of these animals demonstrating any of these behaviors, keep your distance and notify a ranger or your camp host immediately.

Bears

Okay, so I've covered some mean critters, disease-carrying critters, and critters that sometimes carry rabies. Now let's talk about bears. And I don't mean Smokey and Yogi. There are eight species of bear in the world, but only two, the American black bear and the brown bear (grizzly and Kodiak) reside in the United States.

The *American black bear* is the most common bear species and can be found all over North America. Though they usually live in forested areas, they are sometimes spotted in fields and meadows in 40 of our states. The highest concentrations are in the Northeast, the northern Midwest, the Rocky Mountain region, the west coast, and Alaska. And although the majority of them have black fur, their name is misleading because they are also brown, cinnamon, blond, and sometimes white. They range in size depending on their age, health, sex, the season, and area; however, males are typically larger than females with an average weight of 225 pounds.

Black bears are curious, intelligent, shy, mostly solitary scavengers who spend most of their waking hours looking for food. Because they want nothing to do with us, they are more active at night, dusk, and dawn in heavily populated areas; conversely, they're more active during the day in remote locations. Although they will tolerate each other if there is an abundance of food in one area, black bears prefer to be alone unless it's mating season, or during cub rearing years.

They are omnivores, meaning they eat everything, plants *and* animals; specifically plants, fruits, nuts, insects, honey, fish, small mammals, and dead animals. Opportunistic feeders, they are attracted to fish rich habitats, bee-hives, campgrounds, human garbage, pet food, and livestock. And while most bears hibernate, they awaken easily from their dens (caves or hollowed out logs). However, bears in warm climates with access to a consistent food supply don't hibernate at all.

Not long ago, a majestic 300-pound cinnamon colored black bear paid my family a visit while we were camping in Lake Tahoe. We were in our trailer and looked out just in time to see the bear step over my brother in his low one-man tent before he pivoted and parked in front of my sister's tent. Had she unzipped her door at that precise moment, she would have been nose to nose with the bear. We ran out of our trailer, yelling and waving our arms wildly. My niece grabbed a pan and a wooden spoon and came out banging on it. I know it sounds crazy, but if a bear enters your campsite, you're supposed to make yourself as big as possible and make a lot of noises. It worked, and the bear scampered into the next campsite. Which he liked better because it had an unattended, open cooler.

There are two subspecies of *brown bears*, grizzly and Kodiak. The **grizzly bear** is California's state animal and graces the flag, even though they've been extinct in California since 1922.

Today, they can be found roaming dense forests, subalpine meadows, open plains, and arctic tundra in Alaska, Idaho, Wyoming, Washington, and Montana. Grizzlies are often dark brown, black, or light cream, but most of their fur is lighter in color, giving them a grizzled effect. Unlike the American black bear, they have large shoulder humps, a "kinked" facial profile, and much longer (and visible) front claws. They're also larger, weighing 500 pounds, on average.

Like their cousin, the black bear, brown bears are also curious, intelligent, shy, and mostly solitary scavengers. Brown bears have a reputation for being more aggressive though, which is due in part to the way they respond to danger. Simply put, **black bears** tend to **retreat** when feeling threatened, whereas **brown bears** tend to **defend**. For example, because of their hefty size and longer claws, brown bears are not good climbers. So while a female black bear will send her cubs up a tree at the first sign of trouble, a brown bear can't do this, so instead will stand her ground to defend them.

Brown bears are one of the most omnivorous animals in the world, eating the greatest variety of foods of any bear, and despite their reputations, are only 10% carnivorous (meat-eating). Plants, grasses, roots, berries, whitebark pine nuts, and insects comprise most of their diets. Because they are clumsy hunters, their prey often escapes capture. Nevertheless, they occasionally catch and kill young or old mammals because they are slower and weaker (such as deer, moose, caribou, sheep, goats, antelope, bison, and wild boars). They are also light sleepers and opportunistic feeders, and will eat dead animals, prey on small rodents and livestock, and feast at garbage dumps, salmon-rich rivers, honey bee farms, and campsites.

The *Kodiak bear* is the largest subspecies of the brown bear, rivaling the polar bear, which is *the* largest member of the bear family. Bart, the bear who starred in *The Bear, Legends of the Fall*, and *The Edge*, was a Kodiak bear, and he weighed 1,779 lbs. in his prime and was 8'10" tall. Yikes!

Grizzlies and Kodiaks share the same characteristics, diet, and physical appearance, with the only distinguishing difference being their size and location. Because they live on a remote island in Alaska, Kodiaks enjoy a pristine habitat and well-managed fish populations; which, in large part, explains their hefty size. (Kodiak bears weigh 1,200 pounds on average.)

A fed bear is a dead bear

Okay campers, now that I've educated you about bears, it's time for the "Don't feed the bears" lecture. By far the biggest mistake a camper or person living near bears can make is to intentionally or unintentionally feed a bear. Although you may *think* you're doing him a big favor, this act will ultimately lead to the bear's demise. Look, would you continue to eat roots, insects, and raw fish when you could have Oreos, soda, and chips instead? Use your noggin, people. Once a bear gets a taste of "people" food, his fondness for roots, insects, and raw fish wears off. And let's not forget that they're opportunistic (i.e., lazy) hunters and, simply put, your food is often easier to come by than theirs is. So, if you feed one, he'll come back looking for more. And because they scare campers and cause havoc (not to mention severe damage forging through cars and tents, etc.), they ultimately have to be euthanized.

So, heed the warnings and use the bear boxes, never leave food out, and never intentionally feed the bears. And backpackers, suspend your bear-resistant food container 10–15 feet off the ground (and at least four feet from each vertical support). There are no bear boxes in the wilderness, which is a great segue to my next topic.

Camping Safely in Bear Country

If you store your food in a bear box, hard-sided vehicle, or a bear-resistant food container, they won't be attracted to your campsite in the first place. But as I alluded to in Chapter 3, food isn't the only thing that attracts bears. They also like *pet food, pots and utensils, cooking oils, fuel for stoves and lanterns, unopened canned beverages, cosmetics, insect repellents, lotions, toothpaste, and garbage.* Meaning you need to treat these items like food, and lock them up tight, or throw them away in a bear-resistant dumpster.

There are other things you can do besides exercising proper food storage to be safe while backpacking or car camping in bear country, and in a nutshell they are:

1. Don't sleep in the same clothes **that you cooked in**.
2. Keep a flashlight and bear spray with you in the tent at night.
3. Keep pets close (and leashed).
4. Suspend food at least 100 yards away from cooking and food storage areas when backpacking.
5. Avoid aromatic foods such as bacon or fish.
6. Never put food inside your tent.
7. Camp away from trails or berry patches.
8. Pack out all garbage and food scraps.

If a bear enters your camp and you are unable to scare it away, seek shelter because it is most likely "human-habilitated" and "food-conditioned." Simply stated: it's not his first rodeo, and he's not afraid of people anymore.

Bear Attacks

According to a 100-year study documented by Wikipedia, actual attacks on humans resulting in death in the U.S. are rare, (**18** wild **black bear** and **36** wild **brown bear.**) There were also fatalities inflicted by captive bears, but since I'm not worried about you bumping into a caged bear, I've chosen not to include those stats. These numbers don't seem so high when you consider that there were 32 fatalities resulting from dog attacks in 2013 *alone.*

Having said that, if a *black* bear charges, fight back with everything you have (preferably bear spray). But if you don't have bear spray, then use rocks, sticks, or your camera. Don't try to outrun, out swim, or out climb the black bear because they can run up to 35 mph and are excellent swimmers and climbers.

I'll be honest; there's conflicting information about what to do if a *brown* bear attacks. Some people recommend playing dead if a grizzly makes a non-predatory advance (e.g., a mother protecting her cubs), while others think you should fight back. **I'm not qualified to say either way,** so I encourage you to check out the websites that I've referenced at the back of this book. What I do know is this: brown bears are also fast runners and good swimmers, so you cannot out run or out swim them either.

And if you're thinking you could escape one by climbing a tree because they're not good climbers, then think again. It may take a brown bear longer to reach you, but he will.

Big Furry Cats

Though *mountain lions* are solitary animals most active at night, some will venture out during the day in unpopulated areas in pursuit of food. But you won't see one unless it wants you to because these creatures have an extraordinary sense of sight and smell and don't want anything to do with you. Weighing 140 pounds on average, they are the largest wildcat in North America and are identifiable by their tan or reddish brown or gray coats and long tails.

Their name is a little misleading as they live in fourteen states (mostly western), and not all of them are mountainous. Some live in deserts, humid coastal forests, and arid hillsides, and there is a small population in Florida. Deer is their favorite menu choice, but they'll eat any mammals, large or small, and sometimes domestic animals and pets.

If you encounter a mountain lion, pull small children and/ or your dog in close, stay calm, and slowly back way. DO NOT RUN, as this will stimulate the lion's instinct to chase. If he's within 25' and exhibiting aggressive behavior (intense eye contact and crouching), hold your ground. Make yourself as big as possible by opening your jacket if you're wearing one, wave your arms slowly, speak loudly and if possible, throw things at him. If he attacks, fight back. Unlike a bear, the lion will not back off if he thinks you're dead. Oh, and ladies, as if their non-foaming jaws aren't menacing enough, you should know that they sometimes carry rabies. But relax, actual mountain lion attacks on humans are *extremely rare.*

Bobcats are on the move three hours before sunset to midnight and then again before dawn to three hours after sunrise. You might spot one in the middle of the afternoon, but like mountain lions, they're stealthy. They are the most common wildcat in North America and are much smaller than a mountain lion, weighing 21 pounds on average. Distinguishing features are their spotted tan and black coats, broad paws, long legs and cropped tail. They roam almost every state, with the exception of Minnesota, eastern South Dakota, and most of Missouri. Rabbits and hares are their favorite meal choice, but they also eat insects, birds, chickens, small rodents, and sometimes, small pets and deer. They *never* attack people, and rarely carry rabies, so if you see one, consider yourself lucky, but keep your distance.

Big Furry Dogs

A howling pack of *coyotes* might send a shiver up your spine, but don't panic; they're not howling at you, but rather at other packs. Territorial by nature, this is their way of saying, "Hey, this section of the woods belongs to us." They also howl to find each other and to protect their cubs from predators.

Unlike the solitary mountain lion and bobcat, coyotes are pack animals, which live in small family groups. The possibility of spotting one is fairly high as they are active all day but especially at dawn and dusk. Resembling dogs, they have pointed ears, slender muzzles, droopy bushy black-tipped tails, reddish coats, and weigh 42 pounds on average. Coyotes roam every single state except for Hawaii, hunting small mammals (mostly mice, voles, and rabbits).

Shy, but unafraid, they are adaptable, opportunistic creatures of habit, so they will stalk you for your food, especially in areas that people usually camp. Backpackers are more likely than campground campers to encounter a coyote, but it does happen on occasion, so it's important that you store your food properly if you want to avoid these guys. That said, if one does pay you a visit, stay calm. Put yourself between him and your children, grab your dog, and react in the same manner that you would when faced with a mountain lion. (Make yourself bigger, shout, throw stuff, don't run, etc.). Although they rarely attack people, they have been known to attack cats and small dogs. And again, don't forget that coyotes are a common carrier of rabies.

Like coyotes, **wolves** howl and travel in pack families, but unlike coyotes they keep their distance. And though they do howl more when the moon is full (because it's lighter), they don't howl *at* it. They are also most active around dawn and dusk, but hunt day and night.

A mysterious animal and nothing like the predators depicted in the movie *The Grey*, they develop close relationships, strong social bonds, demonstrate deep affection for their families, and form highly structured packs. In this way, they differ from Coyotes, which associate with each other in loose groups.

The largest member of the canine family, wolves resemble a German shepherd or malamute. Some have pure white, brown, gray, cinnamon, or black coats, and they average 80 pounds. The United States wolf population declined dramatically during the mid-1930s, as most of the packs were killed off. But today they roam the wilderness in Alaska, Idaho, Michigan, Minnesota, Montana, Wisconsin, and Wyoming. Their diet consists of large hoofed mammals like elk, deer, moose, and caribou, but they also prey on beavers, rabbits, and other small animals. They rarely attack people; but because they view dogs as competition, keep them close if you're camping in wolf country. And though folks in Europe have encountered rabid wolves, the United States has only reported two over a 100-year period.

Summing Up the Wild Things

So to review, don't pet the critters. Report rabid animal concerns to the camp host or a ranger, and if you lock up your food nice and tight, you shouldn't have any unwanted visitors. And remember, large animals capable of inflicting severe injury, usually do everything in their power to avoid you. So relax, breathe easy and enjoy the wild things and where they are.

Little Critters

I hate critters that crawl, slither or fly, so this was a tough section to write. (I actually taped pieces of paper all over my computer monitor to block out the spider images, etc.) However, I learned a few things, so here is a list of 11 critters to avoid while recreating in their environments:

CRITTER	WHERE IT LIVES	BITE OR STING AFFECTS
Bees, Wasps, Hornets & Yellow Jackets	Beehives or nests	Pain and sometimes death (when allergic).
Black Widow Spiders	Wood piles, under ledges, & plants	Severe cramps, nausea, vomiting, chills, seizure, or rise in blood pressure.
Caterpillars	Trees, shrubs, & plants	Pain, itching, burning, sometimes swelling, numbness, and vomiting.
Chiggers	Grassy fields, forests, & parks	Itchy welts and sometimes infection.
Deer Flies	Wetlands & forests	Pain, sometimes tularemia (an infectious bacterial disease).
Fire Ants	Large mounds in open areas	Severe pain and sometimes death (when allergic).
Fleas	Small mammals	Itching, infection and sometimes bubonic plague.
Mosquitoes	Near still water	Itching, infection, sometimes malaria, yellow fever & West Nile virus, etc.
Scorpions	Under rocks or in bark (etc.)	Pain, swelling, itching, vomiting, vision problems, and sometimes death.
Snakes	Various places	Various affects (explained in the following pages).
Ticks	Grass & plants	None, sometimes Lyme disease, Rocky Mt. spotted fever, or other tick-borne illness.

Bees, Wasps, Hornets, & Yellow Jackets

If a honey bee stings you, it'll lose its stinger and die, but wasps, hornets, and yellow jackets keep their stingers and, for this reason, can inflict multiple stings. A normal reaction is pain, swelling, and redness around the sting site. If these symptoms occur, simply remove the stinger, clean the site, apply ice, and take an oral antihistamine for itching and swelling; and ibuprofen or aspirin for pain.

An allergic reaction (i.e., anaphylactic reaction) will cause facial swelling, wheezing, labored breathing, dizziness, and, a sudden drop in blood pressure. If you have an EpiPen (epinephrine), inject it immediately, call 911 and gently remove the stinger with a sterilized needle or even a credit card. Pay particular attention to the poison sack at the end of the stinger. Do NOT use tweezers, as they squeeze any leftover venom in the stinger into your body.

Black Widow Spiders

Unless you want to get up close and personal with a poisonous black widow spider, stay away from woodpiles and tree stumps, Diva. I've caught my breath on a fair number of tree stumps in the past, but no more. They also like to spin their webs under ledges; and between rocks, and plants. Her long legged, glossy black body and "hourglass" symbol of distinctive orange, red, or yellow on her underside, will give her away. Yep, you read that right; they're not all red.

Black widow spiders are the most venomous spiders in North America, and live on every continent of the world except for

Antarctica. Their bites may cause a stabbing pain in the bite area, but sometimes they're painless. If you think one bit you, look for swelling, one or two red fang marks, redness, and tenderness at the bite site. Severe muscle cramps, nausea, vomiting, chills, seizure, and a rise in blood pressure are bite symptoms, so seek medical attention immediately as there is anti-venom available.

And while we're on the subject, the other two spiders that make the *Three Most Venomous Spiders in the United States* list are the ***Hobo*** and ***Brown Recluse***. Hobo's reside in Washington, Oregon, Idaho, Montana, Wyoming, Utah, and Colorado, and Brown Recluse spiders reside in our southern states. For more information about these too-terrifying-to-write-about little critters, please see Additional Reading, at the back of this book.

Caterpillars

There are roughly ten poisonous caterpillars scooting about the United States, so if you happen upon one that's furry, brightly colored or multi-colored don't touch! These little guys leave painful spines in your skin when they sting, causing at the very least, itching and burning. The best way to remove them is with a piece of tape or Band-Aid. Call the Poison Control Center (800-222-1222) right away if you experience an allergic reaction (swelling, numbness, nausea, or vomiting). And if I've piqued your curiosity about poisonous caterpillars, see the articles I've referenced at the back of this book under resources.

Chiggers

Although these little buggers (i.e., mite larvae) don't carry disease, they are itchy when they attach to your skin. Like ticks, they migrate to warm, moist areas on your body, but unlike ticks, they don't carry disease. They're tiny and barely visible to the naked eye, but in a group, resemble little red bumps on your skin. They thrive throughout the US, most commonly in grassy fields, forests, parks, and gardens, as well as in areas that are moist such as near rivers or lakes. Over the counter, products will help with the itching, but seek medical attention if your skin looks infected or welts appear to be spreading.

Deer Flies

These little bloodsuckers deliver a very painful bite and sometimes carry tularemia (an infectious bacterial disease). They are larger than houseflies but smaller than wasps with beelike abdominal stripes. Most of them are yellow-brown to black with dark bands on their wings, but some are gray. The distinguishing characteristic of a deer fly is their patterned gold or green eyes. Although the majority of people bitten by a deer fly will only feel pain, others experience allergic reactions such as itching and swelling. Watch out if you're planning to camp in Florida because although these flying pests thrive everywhere in the world, the highest concentration resides in the Sunshine State.

Fire Ants

Fire ants look a lot like regular ants, but if one bites you, it'll hurt. Mostly found in the southern states, they produce large mounds in open areas and are aggressive when disturbed.

During an attack, the fire ant latches onto the skin with its jaw, then stings from its abdomen and is capable of injecting venom multiple times. Their stings typically cause red lesions that burn and itch and, sometimes, painful pus-filled lesions. Cold packs, pain relievers, and antihistamines can help relieve the discomfort. A large number of stings may trigger a toxic or severe, life-threatening allergic reaction, and, in this case, you should hightail it to the nearest emergency room or call 911.

Fleas

Although fleas rarely hitch a ride on you and your camping stuff, it's not out of the question. They love mice, rats, chipmunks, squirrels, raccoons, opossums, foxes, skunks, deer, coyotes, bobcats, Florida panthers, and, of course, dogs. So it's possible that one could hop from one of these animals, and then onto you. Some people are very sensitive to flea bites, and excessive scratching can cause a wound or infection. And sometimes they carry bubonic plague (a potentially life-threatening disease). But don't panic, it's pretty rare. According to the Centers for Disease Control, the plague only afflicts on average seven people per year. So use that insect repellent with DEET, and you won't have to worry about the itchy little buggers. And, at the risk of stating the obvious, if you're camping with your four-legged best friend, make sure he wears a new flea and tick collar.

Mosquitoes

Also bloodsuckers, these guys top the *Most Annoying Insects* list, and with good reason. Not only do they itch like crazy when they bite us, but they're *everywhere*. Well, apparently you won't encounter any in Antarctica, but you're their smorgasbord in the rest of the world. And it stands to reason, I guess, that warm, humid regions have them year round while more temperate regions catch a break during the winter months (while they hibernate). And again, as previously stated, some mosquitoes carry yellow fever, malaria, tularemia, West Nile virus, and other infectious diseases, so don't forget the insect repellent, ladies. You're going to need it.

Scorpions

Although there are over 1,500 species of scorpions roaming the globe, only 25 are fatal to humans. Here are five to watch out for, and where in the world you'll find them.

1. *Indian red scorpion*: India, Pakistan, & Nepal
2. *Emperor (aka Imperial) scorpion:* West Africa
3. *Arizona bark scorpion*: Deserts (CA, AZ & Northern Mexico)
4. *Deathstalker scorpion*: North Africa, Middle East, & Sahara Desert
5. *Yellow fat tail scorpion:* North Africa & Southeast Asia

I'm not going to waste everyone's time discussing the scorpions that roam other countries. But you do need to know about the ***Arizona bark scorpion*** if you're planning to camp in the southwest, or in northern Mexico. You do not want to come in contact with one of these little light brown critters because they can be deadly. But if you do, and you experience blurred vision, random eye movements, trouble swallowing, drooling, swelling of the tongue, slurred speech, dizziness, or twitching muscles; seek medical attention immediately.

Snakes

There are roughly 2,900 species of snakes slithering around the world, but relax, only four venomous snakes live in the United States. They are, drum roll, please…rattlesnakes, copperheads, cottonmouths (aka water moccasins), and coral snakes.

Rattlesnakes are responsible for the majority of snakebite fatalities, due in large part to their abundance. You can find one in almost every part of the continental US, but they're especially common in the southwest. Rattlesnakes get their name from the rattles in their tails, which they use to warn people or predators when threatened. Being five feet long on average, they are the largest of the four venomous snakes in the US, ranging in color from brown to gray and have big, thick bodies and triangular heads. Sun worshippers by nature, they can be found soaking in the rays on logs, boulders, or open areas in the mountains, grasslands, scrub brush, swamps, and deserts. Oh, joy.

If you're planning to camp in North Carolina, you'll want to wear boots and watch out for the *copperhead* snakes because this state has the highest incident of venomous snake bites in the United States. Copperheads don't warn before they strike because their strike *is* their warning. But their venom is less potent, and because they rarely release all of it, their bites are seldom lethal. Its copper-colored head and tan hourglass shaped bands on a pinkish background will give it away, and they're not very long (average length is 2 feet). But much like a rattlesnake, they have big, thick bodies. They live in coastal areas, marshes, forests, fields, and wooded parts of hilly and mountainous areas across the eastern states and as far west as Texas.

Like a rattlesnake, the **cottonmouth** snake (aka water moccasin) is named after the way they warn people or predators. When threatened, they open their jaws wide, revealing stark white oral chambers. You'll encounter them in or around water in the southeast, and although their bites are very painful, few have been fatal. Relatively large at an average length of 3 feet, they have striping along the sides of their large triangular heads, are brown or nearly black, and have vague black or dark brown crossbands on their bodies. (Juveniles are bolder in color and have a yellow tail.) And although their natural range is the southeast, they can also be found as far north as the Carolina's and as far west as Kentucky.

The venomous *coral* snake is often confused with the non-venomous scarlet king snake, which has similar color bands. The difference between the two is the arrangement of these bands. *If the red bands are touching the yellow bands,* then it's a coral snake. This popular rhyme will help you remember: *"Red touches yellow, kills a fellow. Red touches black, friend of Jack."* Their size is another way to tell them apart; king snakes are larger (4–5 feet long), whereas the average coral snake is around two feet long. They reside in our southern states (Alabama, Arizona, Florida, Louisiana, Mississippi, North Carolina, and Texas) and hang out in rotting leaf piles, wood, and tree stumps.

Snake Bite First Aid

Though these snakes will do everything in their power to get away before you reach them, you should know that, if bitten, all four have different symptoms and consequences. For example, a copperhead snake might not kill you, but if the bite is left untreated, it will cause extensive scarring and possible paralysis of the inflicted limb.

That said, if you know for sure that a poisonous snake bit you, call an ambulance, or if you have a driver, hightail it to the nearest emergency room. But call ahead to let them know you're coming so that they will have the anti-venom ready. While you wait for the ambulance, or while driving the victim to the emergency room do this:

1. Stay calm and keep as still as possible.
2. Keep the affected area **below heart level** to reduce the flow of venom.
3. Remove rings or constricting items because the affected area may swell.
4. If possible, make a loose splint to help restrict movement of the area.
5. If there are signs of shock (paleness, rapid, shallow breathing or cold, clammy skin), lay the person flat, raise the feet about a foot and cover them with a blanket.

Contrary to popular belief, DO NOT:

1. Cut into a snakebite with a knife or razor.
2. Try to suck out the venom by mouth.

3. Apply a cold compress to the snakebite.

4. Give the victim any medications, food, or water.

5. Raise the site of the bite above the level of the person's heart.

And don't waste your time trying to capture and kill the snake that bit you or your friend, because snakes **can bite in reflex even after they're dead** (oh my God). If possible, get a good look, but keep your distance. Also, don't wash the bite area, as this will make it harder for medical professionals to identify the snake in question. It's also a good idea to call the Poison Control Center, especially if you panic and forget what you've just read. (Which could happen.)

Ticks

These little freeloaders hang out in grass and plants, jumping on unsuspecting people and animals as they pass. They literally get under your skin after traveling to a warm, moist location on your body, usually, armpits or the groin area. Yikes! Most tick bites aren't life threatening, but some carry Lyme disease, and Rocky Mountain spotted fever. That said, the infected tick can't spread illness unless it attaches to you for 36 hours, so it's important that you inspect your body carefully after spending time in grassy or wooded areas. To prevent them from jumping on you in the first place, keep your arms, legs, and head covered, and again, don't forget the insect repellant.

But if you find that one of these little buggers has attached itself to you, it's critical that you remove it properly. I pulled the following information off the CDC's website (Center for Disease

Control & Prevention). So, if you'd like even more information about ticks and other disease carrying critters, then please take a moment to visit *cdc.gov*.

To remove a tick:

1. Use fine-tipped tweezers to grasp the tick as close to the skin's surface as possible.
2. Pull upward with steady, even pressure. Don't twist or jerk the tick; this can cause the mouthparts to break off and remain in the skin. If this happens, remove the mouthparts with tweezers. If you are unable to remove the mouth with clean tweezers, leave it alone and let the skin heal.
3. Once you've removed the tick, thoroughly clean the bite area and your hands with rubbing alcohol, an iodine scrub, or soap and water.

Insect Bite Relief

The insect bite relief products mentioned in Chapter 3 will soothe a bee sting, and the bites of chiggers, fire ants, deer flies, mosquitoes, and spiders. But again, you'll have to seek medical attention if you have an allergic reaction to a bee sting, caterpillar, black widow spider, or Arizona bark scorpion bite.

Poison Ivy, Oak & Sumac

These poisonous plants won't kill you in the literal sense, but you'll end up pleading for mercy if you come in contact with one. The medical term for the red, itchy, bumpy rash that develops is *contact dermatitis,* which is an allergic reaction to the oil *urushiol* found in the plants. It spreads through direct contact (brushing up against it as you pass) or indirect contact (clothing, sports gear, gardening tools, or pet fur, etc.).

Description/Region

There are two basic types of **poison ivy**, climbing, and non-climbing. Both types have three broad, densely "haired" leaves, or leaflets, with different textures and colors depending on the season or location. The small, lightly colored tan or light yellow berries and the popular rhyme, *"Leaves of three? Let them be"* will help you identify this plant. It climbs creeps and clumps in bush form, and thrives on the edges of fields, forests, parking lots, or roads. You'll find it east of the Rocky Mountains, but also throughout most of the continental US (the far west, deserts, and high altitudes being the exceptions).

Poison oak thrives wherever there are oak trees. In the eastern region, it looks a lot like poison ivy while out west it's more shrub-like, has hairless leaflets, and is capable of climbing up to 8 feet.

Poison sumac or swamp sumac (aka poison elder, poison ash, poison dogwood, and poison thunderwood) is considered by many to be the most poisonous plant species in the United States. It looks a lot different than poison ivy or oak (each stem has 7–13 leaflets in pairs) and its more tree-like, growing 6–25 feet tall. And as the name suggests, you'll find it in very wet, swamp-like soils in the eastern Unites States and Canada.

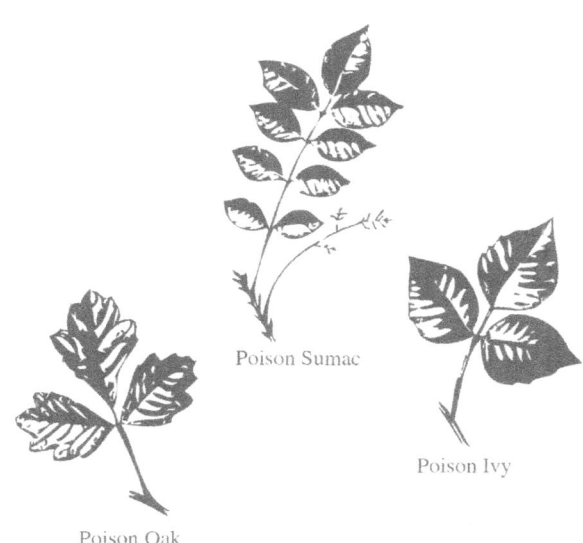

Poison Sumac

Poison Ivy

Poison Oak

Prevention

Of course, the best prevention is avoidance, so it's important that you can identify poison ivy, oak, and sumac. As a precaution, pick up a "barrier cream" such as *Ivy Block* or *Stokoguard* because these creams help prevent rashes before they start. But if you're not wearing a barrier cream, you can still avoid an outbreak if you act within 10–30 minutes by washing the exposed area with cold water, rubbing alcohol or vinegar. (Don't use hot water or soap because the hot water will open your pores, and the soap will spread the oil around.) *Tecnu Extreme Medicated Scrub* or *Zanfel Wash* are also effective at removing the urushiol from your skin. But if you don't have any cleansing products, an aluminum-based deodorant (most are), will at least stop the spread.

Symptoms

Everyone is allergic to poison ivy, oak, and sumac; however, some are more allergic than others. A normal reaction includes itching, red streaks, a general redness where the plant brushed against the skin, and small bumps, hives, or blisters. A severe reaction includes swelling of the face (eyelids may swell shut), mouth, neck, or genitals, and widespread, large blisters that ooze a lot of fluid. Yikes. It usually lasts three weeks, but it takes a day or two for the symptoms to appear. (Although it could take just a few hours; or 7-10 days.)

Treatment

Prevention tactics aside, if you end up with *contact dermatitis,* you're going to have to wait it out. You can get temporary relief from mild cases by taking a very hot shower, or by spraying the exposed area with deodorant. But an anti-itch lotion such as *Sumactin* or *Calamine lotion* will do a better job soothing irritated skin. More severe cases will require a trip to the doctor for some corticosteroid pills or shots.

CHAPTER 5 TIPS

- ✓ Download the Critter Lookup app to identify various insects, reptiles, birds, small, medium and large mammals. This free app is a wealth of information and operates on all Apple devices (iOS 5.0 or later).

- ✓ Before you leave for that camping trip, add the Poison Control Centers phone number (800-222-1222) to your phone's contact list, just in case you need it.

- ✓ A portable bug zapper for your campsite will help keep mosquitoes, etc., at bay. (I like the Stinger Cordless Rechargeable Insect Zapper Lantern, which is available from Amazon.)

- ✓ The easiest way to remove a tick is with a "tick key." REI sells them, so if you're camping in a tick-infested area, then it might be wise to pick one up.

- ✓ Don't burn poison ivy, oak, or sumac because it can cause a severe allergic reaction when ingested into your lungs.

Six

Camping With Children & Dogs

July 7, 2009
<u>Emerald Bay, Lake Tahoe</u>
  Last night's slumber party with the kids was so fun!
  Never heard so many giggles coming from the other
  side of our tent trailer.

I know I'm a little biased, but if you do it correctly, there's no better way to bond with your family then gathered around a campfire, under a starry sky. My nieces and nephews are part of my favorite camping memories, and I smile every time we pass the large boulder where they danced, singing, "Hey, hey, we're the Monkees!" And I can't gaze into a campfire without remembering the night my husband told them his cheesy *Captain Jack* story about a vindictive, one-legged caretaker. It wasn't very scary, but his enthusiasm was so contagious they went along with him, just for the fun of it. Seriously, does it get better than that?

Nevertheless, if you plan to embark on a camping adventure with your children or dog, it's important to be prepared so that everyone will be…I can't believe I haven't said this yet—*happy campers.*

WITH CHILDREN

The key to a successful camping trip with your kids is having plenty of activities on hand to keep them entertained. Your little Einstein might enjoy collecting bugs, tracking paw prints, or stargazing. And your little athletes might enjoy bike riding, frolicking in the water, or playing a group sport. My point is, whatever their interest, the outdoors has something for every kid. The young ones—*and* the old ones.

It's also important to choose a campsite near the restrooms, and a campground that offers watercraft rentals, bike riding, and a little general store. That way you're covered if you forget to pack something, or you need more wine. (I'm joking.)

ACTIVITIES
Bike Riding

A bike ride is a great way for the entire family to explore the campground *and* get a little exercise. But before you go to the trouble of finding the helmets and hitching the bikes to your bike rack, make sure this activity is on the amenity list under your campground's "Description." For example, Eagle Point Campground in Lake Tahoe doesn't list this activity as an amenity because the campground has steep hills.

Campground APPs

I love trivia, and I can't think of a better time to enjoy it than by the light of the silvery moon...or a campfire. The *Animal Fun Facts 1000* app is an excellent way to learn about the animals you're camping with (and others), and it has lots of cool, interesting, and bizarre facts. As of April 22, 2014 it's free, but it may have a small price tag by the time you read this. The app requires iOS 6.0 or later and is compatible with iPhone, iPad, and iPod touch.

You can make up your scary stories as you go along like my husband does, or you could download *Coleman's Creepy Campfire Tales*. It's a fun app with a collection of age-appropriate stories for kids, teens, and adults to read around the campfire. Some of the stories even have scary sound effects to make the creepy tales even creepier. The app is free, requires iOS 2.2 or later, and is compatible with iPhone, iPad, and iPod touch.

If you pay attention, you'll probably spot some animal tracks while recreating in their backyard. So if you and your children want to figure out which animal made them, check out *My Nature Animal Tracks*. This app has consistently been on the Top 100 Reference Apps List in iTunes. It features an extensive, easily searchable database of full-color digital images of tracks and the animal that made them. It'll work on your Apple device (requires iOS 3.0 or later) or Android and costs $7 or $5.

Even if your kids have zero interest in astronomy, they'll love the *Star Walk, by Vito Tech* app. It's an interactive guide that uses your phone or tablet's built-in GPS to show constellations, planets, and stars. For example, Cancer (the crab) is a constellation, and when you hold it up to the sky you'll see a giant crab (among other things) lit up by stars. It's so cool. It's also affordable at $3, and compatible on iPhone, iPad, Android, Kindle, and Windows phones.

Fishing

Fishing can be an enjoyable activity for the entire family, but don't forget to purchase a license for each fisherperson; otherwise, you could be fined by the game warden. And as always, the amount varies from state to state, but in California fines start at $100. Zebco makes a fun little fishing "pole" for kids, so if this activity appeals to you, check out *Zebco's Spincast Fishing Combo w/ Tackle Pak.* It includes a 202 reel, a 5'6" rod, and tackle wallet, gets a respectable 4.2 stars from Amazon users, and is affordable at $20.

Games

Let's face it, you and your family can only stare at the stars and each other for so long, which is why you should pack a few games. You probably have your favorite "go to" board games, but if you feel like surprising your family with something new,

Game/Toys	Rating	Price
"Hit the Trail" Card Game	5.0	$12.99
Roll Up Campground Magnetic Darts	5.0	$19.95
Educational Outdoors/Camp Board Game	5.0	$24.99
Night Sky Playing Cards	4.5	$ 5.95
Coghlan's Kids Collapsible Mesh Insect House	5.0	$ 3.99
Coghlan's The Original Audubon Birdcall 4 Kids	4.0	$ 7.99
Wabobo Pro Extreme Water Bouncing Ball	5.0	$ 9.99
Stream Machine 36" Water Gun	4.7	$19.99

then check out some of these camping specific and sometimes educational games and toys. (All of which are for sale on Amazon or Campmor.)

Badminton, volleyball, croquet, horseshoes, soccer, Twister, and *flag football* are also fun games to play while camping (provided there is enough space in your campsite, of course).

Hiking

Hiking is a fun family activity, but unless you're planning to hit the trail carrying your baby in a papoose-style sling, you should consider a "baby backpack." I like the *Osprey Poco Plus Child Carrier* because it's comfortable, sturdy, and most of all—safe for baby *and* you. Amazon customers give it a 4.8 rating, and it sells for $260.

Beautiful scenery and good company aside, it doesn't take long for young children and teens to get bored. The simple game "I Spy" should entertain youngsters for a while *and* keep them engaged in their surroundings. Then again, if you want to take that game to the next level, download the free Project Noah app to your Android or iPhone. It identifies *and* documents the wildlife, which is fun to review when you get back to camp.

However, you'll need a more sophisticated approach when entertaining those teens on the trail. So if you have a GPS or smartphone, hand it over and let them navigate a geocache (a GPS treasure hunt.) I'll expand more on this topic in Chapter 7.

And parents don't forget the hats, sunscreen, bug repellent, water, and snacks. You're going to need them!

Movie Night

We have a large 72" screen and movie projector that we like to take when we're camping with our family and friends because, well, there's something magical about watching a movie under the stars. The key to this working, of course, is taking the right equipment (screen, projector, generator, and a long extension cord). You'll also need a large campsite that flanks the woods so that you can park the generator there. My husband groans every time I break out the big screen, but our fellow campers love it. Oh, and if you're feeling nostalgic, whip out the Jiffy Pop! It's perfect for camping because you can cook it over a campfire, and it comes in its own self-contained, disposable pan.

Scavenger Hunt

Your kids will forget all about their phones if you send them out on a good old-fashioned scavenger hunt. Of course, if they're little they'll need a chaperone; however, the older ones can go it alone, and will be entertained for hours. Here's a list of possible items for a campground hunt, but I'm sure you can come up with more.

1. 12" Pinecone
2. Piece of bark
3. Two leafs that look alike
4. Flower
5. Something that starts with a b
6. Something red

I like scavenger hunts in general, but I'm particularly fond of the *digital* variety. And they're especially fun for children because they motivate them to discover things, and engage in activities that they otherwise might not. To give you an idea of what I mean, I gave this list to my nieces and nephews a few years back.

Take a picture of. . .
1. Three of you sitting on the mansion steps.
2. A canoe or kayak.
3. Someone jumping off the pier.
4. A female in uniform.
5. "Old Mercury."
6. A chipmunk or squirrel.
7. A 12" pinecone.
8. The #52 campsite sign.
9. A Coleman tent trailer.
10. A "Dogs Must Be on Leash" sign.
11. One of you shaking the camp hosts hand.
12. Three of you at the amphitheater.
13. A red tent.
14. A dog.

We were at Sugar Pine State Park, and although we'd camped there a few times, they hadn't paid much attention to the historic buildings at Pine Lodge. So on this day, they got a better view of the mansion and focused for a moment at least on "Old Mercury," (a historic boat). And, best of all, it was so much fun looking at their pictures when they got back.

Water Activities

If you're lucky, or strategic enough to have a lake nearby, you'll have plenty to do. A lot of lakes within or near popular campgrounds rent various watercraft, so check before you go. Look for the following: canoe, catamaran, jet ski, kayak, paddleboat, stand up paddleboard, sailboat, ski boat, and rowboat rentals.

However, if there are no watercraft rentals, then consider taking along a floating island, inner tubes, rafts, or an inflatable rowboat. Speaking of which, if you're interested, take a look at the *Intex Explorer 200 Boat Set,* which I found on Amazon. It's an affordable, sturdy, two-person inflatable rowboat that gets a 4.1 rating and sells for $20. (Costco also sells water toys in their seasonal section.)

Babies

I love babies, I do, but I don't love them when they're wailing all night from *a flimsy little no-insulation-whatsoever-to-muffle-the-wailing tent.* My husband and I (along with one hundred other campers) had the misfortune of being in the same loop with an unhappy baby one summer night, and it was not pleasant. I'm not exaggerating when I say that this child wailed from the time the sun went down until it came up again. Everyone looked like walking zombies the next day.

Here's the thing: once the majority of campers have retired for the evening, the campground gets library quiet. So when a camper coughs or unzips his or her tent, you hear it. Apparently, someone complained to the camp host the night before we arrived, but what was he supposed to do about it? Kick out the baby and his parents? Honestly, you'd think people would bring their common sense with them when they camp, but sadly, some don't.

So, the moral of this story is: if your little one is under two, just think long and hard about whether or not he or she is mature enough for a campout. Heck, I know a lot of adults who aren't mature enough. Which reminds me, I've spent over two hundred nights in various campgrounds, and I only have one wailing baby story, but I have *numerous* stories about unruly adults. So there's that.

Shower Bags

When your little campers reek like a bear, it's time to hit the showers. Now if you're unprepared, you could spend an hour rummaging through your SUV or tent searching for all the shower paraphernalia. Which is fine, if that's the way you want to spend your vacation; *or* you could create individual *"shower bags"* before you leave home. Trust me, a little preparation will save you a lot of time and aggravation when it's time to wash the outdoors off your children. So before you go, grab some plastic grocery bags with handles from your pantry and pack each bag with the following items:

1. Clean towel/washcloth.
2. Travel size shampoo/conditioner.
3. Travel size bar soap.
4. Cheap rubber flip-flops.
5. Ziploc bag with 10–12 quarters.

6. A clean change of clothes.

You might want to skip the shampoo and conditioner for the kids if you're only camping for a day or two because as my friend Julie so eloquently stated, "Clean bodies, great. Clean hair can wait." Dry shampoo will usually, do the trick here. But if shampoo is necessary, a leave-in conditioner is a good way to speed up the process and save a little money. (Yep, most campground showers are coin operated, so you have to pay for the water.)

Kid Stuff

Don't forget to pack these items for your munchkins before setting off into the wild.

1. Appropriate shoes
2. Beach towels
3. Bikes/helmets
4. Camera
5. Duffle bag
6. DVD player/movie
7. Extra socks
8. Favorite doll or stuffed animal
9. First aid kit
10. Fishing rod(s), etc.
11. Flashlights
12. Games
13. GPS/geocache trinket
14. HandiWipes
15. Insect repellent
16. Paper/pens

17. Picnic basket
18. Shower bags
19. Sippy cups
20. Sleeping bags/pillow
21. S'more ingredients/tools
22. Snacks
23. Sun protection
    - glasses
    - hats
    - sunscreen
24. Swimsuits
25. Walkie Talkies
26. Warm clothing
    - beanies
    - jackets
    - sweatshirts
27. Water accessories
    - arm floats (etc.)
    - goggles
    - inner tubes/rafts
    - life vests

WITH DOGS

I'm a dog person. I'm also a kid person, but we don't have any of those, which means we like to camp with our dogs because, well, they're our family. We enjoy camping with them, and they enjoy camping with us. Of course, I can't read their minds, but I do know unadulterated joy when I see it. I guess the vertical jumps, happy barks, tail wags, and smiles kind of give them away. Still, we understand that people don't love our dogs as much as we do, so we keep a very short leash on them when we camp.

For the most part, campgrounds have the same rules pertaining to man's best friend. In short, they are:

Rules & Regulations

1. You cannot leave them unattended.
2. They must be on a leash in common areas.
3. They must be on a tether (i.e., long lead) in your campsite.
4. You have to pick up their poop.
5. Sometimes there are breed and size restrictions.

1) Leaving Your Dog Unattended

Some folks tie their dogs up in their campsite or leave them in their cars for a while, but that's just mean (not to mention dangerous). Besides, why bring your furry friend in the first place if you're just going to leave him behind? Most dogs will protest loudly, drowning out the breeze rustling through the trees or the joyful chirping of little birds, with their brokenhearted barks and, or howls. And locking your dog in your RV or car is not smart, especially if it's a hot summer day. To illustrate my point, I pulled this information from a study conducted by Jan Null, Adjunct Professor of Meteorology at San Francisco State University.

Cars interior temperature on a 90° day.

Minutes	Temperature
After 10	109°
After 20	119°

After 30	124°
After 60	133°
After 90	138°

As you can see, the temperature rises quicker than you might think. While there are no actual statistics (because people don't tend to report these cases), police estimate that several hundred dogs die in cars each summer from heat exhaustion. And it's a slow, agonizing death. If you don't believe me, try sitting in a 138° car wearing a fur coat, and let me know how you feel. Sorry, that sounded hostile. And don't *even* get me started on children and hot cars. Can you tell I'm passionate about this subject?

Now there are exceptions to the "no leaving dogs unattended in your campsite" rule, but don't tell the camp host or ranger I said that. When we first started camping with our Weimaraner, Cole, we couldn't venture 10 feet away from our tent trailer without him howling bloody murder. But toward the end of his life, he was too old and too tired to protest, so we could sneak away for an hour or so without the whole campground knowing he was there. Still, we only did this after opening all of our trailers windows for cross ventilation, and when the outside temperature was under 70°.

2) The Leash/Lead Rule

There are many reasons why dogs are required to wear a leash in public. Mostly because bad dog owners of ghosts past have ruined it for all good dog owners, present, and future. It's that simple. But whatever the reasons, your dog has to be leashed in the campground's common areas, even *if* he is the teacher's pet in obedience school. Although our rescue, Zoe, would never dream of biting someone, she makes some people nervous, so we snap on her leash when we're in a public place. Are you with me here? It's not to contain Zoe; it's to contain other people's anxiety.

3) The Tethered Rule (in campsite)

Ditto what I said in the last paragraph pertaining to the lease law and keeping your dog close, now let's add critters and bears to the explanation. Imagine this: *You and your family are enjoying your S'mores around the campfire when, all of a sudden your best friend sees something fun like I don't know…a chipmunk, squirrel, raccoon, or God forbid a bear. Before you can open your mouth to say "Stay!" he takes off (because that's what dogs do), and mayhem ensues.*

Now, it's not the end of the world if he takes off after a chipmunk or squirrel. Assuming, that is, he doesn't get so far from camp he can't find his way back or gets hit by a passing car. But if he takes off after a raccoon or bear, then his chances of surviving are slim to none. I'll spare you the gory details, but you don't want to witness your dog wrestling with a raccoon or bear. He won't win.

4) The Poop Rule

For the life of me, I can't figure out why this rule is so difficult for people to understand. If picking up your dog's poop is "below you," you shouldn't own a dog. It's not our favorite thing to do, but they will eventually be banned from public places if people don't abide by this simple rule. So you're ready for nature's call, pick up one of those nifty little poop bag dispensers that clip onto your dog's leash. They're relatively inexpensive at around $12, and you can pick one up at any pet supply store.

5) Breed & Size Restrictions

And finally, before you start packing up your furry friends belongings, check to make sure there aren't any breed or size restrictions at the campground you're planning to visit. Although we've never experienced this, I understand that some ban "aggressive" breeds. (Chow chows, doberman pinchers, German shepherds, huskies, pit bulls, rottweilers; and sometimes Alaskan malamutes, dalmatians, and great danes.) Which is ridiculous, in my opinion, but this book isn't about dog breed discrimination, so that's all I'll say about *that*. While you're at it, make sure there aren't any weight restrictions. We've never come across this either, but I hear some campgrounds only allow small dogs.

Dog Stuff

Don't forget to leave room in your vehicle for your dog if you're planning to take him along. We almost forgot to do this once, which is silly I know, but hey, I've done worse. That said, here's a list of things you'll **definitely** need and a few things that you *might* need for your four-legged camper:

1. *Beds*
2. **Bowls** (food & collapsible water)
3. *Brush*
4. *Doggie Backpack*

5. **Food**
6. *Kennel*
7. **Leashes/Leads**
8. *Life Vests*
9. **Poop bags**
10. *Rug*
11. **Tether system**
12. *Toy*
13. *Treats*
14. **Wipes**

The "Bs"... Bed, Bowls, & Brush

If your dog wasn't kennel trained and would never dream of hanging out in one, you might want to take his dog *bed*. But if you do, put it on a large outdoor rug, so it doesn't get too dirty. Also, you'll need one *bowl* for the campsite and a collapsible bowl for your daypack (unless you plan on giving him water from your canteen). And as a precaution, you might want to take a dog *brush* in case he gets a burr stuck in his fur while hiking, or to remove excess sand he brings back from the beach.

Doggie Backpack

I'll be honest. We don't own one of these backpacks, but every time we pass a dog wearing one, we wish we did. Our running joke is that we'd make our dogs carry everything, but in reality, the compartments are only large enough for their treats, collapsible dog bowl, and water (etc.). I'm not going to recommend a particular one because there are various sizes and types, but Amazon has a good selection if this is something you think your dog would tolerate.

Food

Naturally you know to pack your dog's food, but what isn't so obvious is the means by which to carry and store it. I've seen big bags of dog food in campsites taking up unnecessary space and attracting critters, so before you leave, I recommend that you purchase a plastic storage bin with a lid and handle on top. (Target and Walmart sell them for around $6.) Then, measure out the exact amount you'll need, plus one, and fill it with the food, treats, bowls, and toys if they'll fit. The handle will make it easier to transport, and the lid will prevent critters and your dog, from helping themselves.

Kennel or Tent

If your dog *is* kennel trained, taking it along will make your life a whole lot easier and his more comfortable. First, he can travel in it, which is always a good idea because it will keep him contained, but also he'll feel safe and secure during those down times. But if you don't have a kennel, then you might want to consider a *Mighty Mite Super Set Up Dog Tent* for the campsite. It's soft-sided, so it packs easily, is lightweight and super easy to set up (since there are no threading poles, it's up in 10 seconds flat). Best of all, it's stable. They come in three sizes with prices ranging from $75 to $85, so if you're interested, visit *mightymitedoggear.com* for additional information.

Leash (aka lead)

I'm not going to recommend a particular leash, but I will say this. Campgrounds are pretty strict about the "maximum 6-foot length" rule, so if you own one of those long, retractable leads, you should probably leave it home. Or not, it's your call.

Life Vest

Not all dogs love water, so if yours falls into this category, but you want to take him along on a boat ride, then consider picking up a doggie life vest. Our Weimaraner wore his like a badge of honor. And in addition to being buoyant, they also have handy straps on top, which made lifting him in and out of our canoe a whole lot easier.

Poop Bags

We tried buying cheap bags but stopped once we figured out we were using two per pick-up. That said, you can find sturdy bags on sale if you're willing to do a little shopping. The *Poop Bag Shop* (via Amazon) sells 700 durable, premium bulk refill rolls with a bone shaped dispenser for a mere $18 (which is an excellent deal). Of course, this offer might not be available as you're reading this, but you get my point.

Rugs

Rugs are always helpful when camping, but they are particularly useful when camping with children and dogs. Designate a large rug or mat as the "no shoe zone" for game playing, lounging, or stargazing. We've entertained our nieces and nephews on our large 8' X 10' rug. And, when we're camping with our dogs, it's the perfect place for their beds. Home Depot (and sometimes Costco) sells inexpensive, flexible mats that roll up and are perfect for camping.

Tether System (i.e., Tie Outs)

In order to adhere to the "dogs must be tethered in the campsite rule" you're going to need a good, sturdy tie out for your dog and something to anchor it to. That said, take a look at Amazon's *Dogit Cork-Screw Dog Tie-Out Stake.* It gets a 4.1 rating and costs $7. *Boss Pet* sells a variety of tie outs made from heavy-duty galvanized cable with clips at each end. Prices vary depending on the weight and length, but on average they cost around $14.

Personally, I prefer a tangleless overhead tether system because it allows our dogs to move about the campsite without dragging me, our guests, camp chairs, etc., as they go. But for this system to work, you need two appropriately spaced trees to hook the horizontal line to, and then a vertical line that slides back and forth with your dog. If this system appeals to you, take a look at *PetCo's Dog Tie-Out Trolley.* It's a complete, heavy-duty, and adjustable length system that sells for around $35.

Toys & Treats

Although your dog will think he died and went to heaven when he's vacationing with you, it's always wise to take along a toy or two to keep him entertained during those down times. We pack a couple rawhides and a ball for those rare occasions when we come across a designated off-leash area for dogs. And don't forget the treats for the hiking trail, or to reward him for being good.

Wipes

Let's face it, camping can be a dirty business for us, but it's especially dirty for our dogs. So don't forget the dog wipes. These little wonders—advertised as the "in-between wash"—are perfect for camping. I wipe our dogs down at the end of every camp day, and it helps minimize the amount of dirt that ends up in our trailer. *Natures Miracle* has a good selection; just make sure that the wipes you choose are breed appropriate, as some wipes are smaller than others.

Other dog wipes worth mentioning are *GNC's Dog Essentials Dog Insect Repellant Wipes*, which might be a good backup to your standard regimen. (Or if you don't typically use flea and tick prevention products where you live.) They're formulated to repel fleas and ticks using citronella oil and other natural ingredients and are safe for your dog's entire body. PetSmart sells them for $10, or if you prefer, you can go directly to GNC's website to order them.

CHAPTER 6 TIPS

✓ Parents, choose a campground that's not too far away. You don't want your kids to be tired and cranky before you even get there.

✓ Take along *The Play & Freeze Ice Cream Maker* sold on Amazon and Bed, Bath & Beyond. It's perfect for camping; just toss the ball around for 20 minutes and—voila! Ice cream!

✓ Kids love flashlights, so pack one per child, so they each get to carry their own.

✓ You rookie campers should probably leave pets home until you work out all your camping kinks.

✓ *MightyMiteDogGear.com* has a great selection of gear for your dog (such as tick removers, cooling vests, coats, and a lot more), so check them out.

Seven

Take a Hike

May 12, 1997
<u>**Sequoia National Park**</u>
**If a Diva falls in a forest and no one is around to
hear it, does she make a sound?**

Come on, ladies, you're already there. You know, in that mysterious place called nature, so you might as well become one with it. Hiking can be fun, and it's an excellent way to see the sights *and* get a little exercise. The key is choosing the right hiking trail. If you're new to this activity, you're going to want to skip the 16-mile hike to Half Dome in Yosemite. That said, there are plenty of beginner trails within this national treasure (and in your state).

Now, let me clarify. When I say beginner trails, I mean short trails that are clearly marked, with little or no change in elevation. Whatever you do, do *not* let Tarzan take you off the beaten path. Mine did this once, and I still haven't forgiven him for it. (I fondly refer to this hike as "the time you tried to kill me hike.") Things took a turn for the worst shortly after we stepped off the trail. I ended up walking through a giant spider web, almost colliding with a large poison oak bush, and—for my grand finale—sliding my way down a steep, rocky slope. I was lucky to escape that adventure with just a few scrapes and bruises.

Apps

Map My Hike GPS is a useful app that gives trail details such as elevation changes, etc. and tracks your average pace, distance covered, and calories burned. And its nifty journal feature allows hikers to take notes for future use (or when you're back at the campsite reflecting on how awesome you are). But the icing on the cake is that it's free for everyone. Well, to Android and Apple users that is.

The *SAS Survival Guide,* considered by many to be the best survival reference book ever written, is now available for download to your smartphone. This app is a wealth of information that could be quite useful if you get injured or lost. There are two versions to choose from, the entire book app for $5.99 or the free "lite" app. The latter provides survival basics like how to build a fire, find water, and navigate by the stars, and should be sufficient for a day hike or backpacking trip.

Day Hikes

Generally speaking, there are three types of hikes: easy, moderate, and strenuous. Criteria for determining the various levels are distance, elevation changes, and terrain. Although most fall under the day hike category, they don't typically take a full day to navigate. But as previously stated in Chapter 1: Backpacking, hiking miles are more strenuous than typical walking miles, so just keep this in mind when you choose a trail.

Daypack Supplies

Now, unless you choose a paved "hiking" trail, you're going to need to travel with some stuff. I put hiking in quotes because paved trails aren't hiking trails in the true sense of the word; they're more like shared, all-purpose roads for strolling or bike riding (etc.). Which is fine, I'm down with that, but the only supplies you'll need for one of these strolls is a camera, comfortable shoes, some sunscreen, and maybe a hat. On the other hand, if you're planning to embark on something more strenuous, then you'll need to fill the daypack I discussed in Chapter 3 with most of these items:

1. Navigation device/map
2. Pocketknife
3. Light source
4. Fire starter
5. Emergency Mylar blanket
6. Rain poncho
7. Sunscreen
8. First aid supplies
9. Nutrition
10. Hydration
11. Bear bell/spray

Of course, number 11 only applies when hiking in bear country, and I'm not going to waste any more of your time covering items 1–7 because I've already done that in Chapter 3. But I will say this. The *Emergency Zone Deluxe Survival Bottle Kit* highlighted under Emergency Gear for Car/RV Campers contains most of the items on this list.

First Aid

The first aid kit I recommended for backpackers in Chapter 3 is an excellent option. Then again, if you'd rather make your own, don't forget these items.

1. Adhesive tape
2. *After Bite*
3. Antihistamines
4. Antiseptic wipes
5. Bandages
6. Dressing pads
7. Gauze roll
8. Ibuprofen
9. Moleskin
   (see Chapter Tips)
10. Tweezers

Nutrition

You'll be surprised by how much of an appetite you work up when you're trekking through the boonies. So don't skip the trail mix, energy bars, or snacks just because you had a big breakfast. Besides, you'll need something to munch on while you're waiting for Search and Rescue. Just kidding, but better safe than sorry.

Hydration

Water is the heaviest thing in your daypack, but it's also the most important thing. The amount you'll need to consume to stay hydrated depends on a few things, but mostly on climate and exertion level. Generally speaking, you'll need to pack one liter of water per hour. We took along a water filter when we hiked the 16 miles to Half Dome and back because we didn't want to carry 16 liters of water. Yep, that was an 8-hour hike.

Geocaching

Geocaching is a real-world, outdoor treasure hunting game using GPS-enabled devices. Participants navigate to a particular set of GPS coordinates and then attempt to find a container (cache) hidden at that location. There are different types of caches, with various things inside, but at the very least you'll find a log to sign. Some have trinkets to swap, and the rule is that you can take something, as long as you replace it with something of greater or equal value.

In my mind, the best part of Geocaching is the act of discovering things along the way that you normally wouldn't see. For example, I've probably walked past a dilapidated chimney in Sugar Pine State Park fifty times, and only recently discovered there is a hidden cache inside. Often, their hiding places are scenic or historical, and sometimes, as in the case of the chimney, they are right under your nose.

There are a few companies (i.e., websites) that manage said Geocaches; however, *Geocaching.com* is the largest (with over 1.8 million). Their site is easy to navigate, and they have fun instructional videos, which are a quick way to figure out how things work. To summarize, you need to create an account, choose a cache to locate, download it to your GPS device, and then find it. Once found, sign the log inside the cache, return it to its hiding place, and then enter the find on the website when you get home.

So, if the idea of a GPS treasure hunt appeals to you, purchase or borrow a GPS device, or download one of *Geocaching.com's* apps to your smartphone. Any GPS will work, but if you don't already own one, then take a look at *Magellan's eXplorist GC*. This nifty little device has built-in caches (meaning they don't need to be downloaded from a geocache website before you go). Amazon users give it a 3.4 rating, and it sells for $125.

Safety

I did some research on hiking related rescues and was surprised to learn how often they occur. To give you an idea of what I mean, the search and rescue personnel in Yosemite National Park respond to, on average, 250 calls for help during a typical summer. That's a lot. So, tell someone where you're going, and when you expect to be back so that rescue crews can find you if you're unable to call for help. Better yet, check your phone's coverage map (or take an emergency call device) so that you can make the call yourself. That said, if you do the following, you shouldn't have to be rescued in the first place:

1. Wear appropriate clothing and hiking boots.
2. Stock your daypack with the items previously discussed.
3. Don't stray from the trail.
4. Always be aware of your surroundings.
5. Stay together—no matter what.

The last few items on this list remind me of a story I heard a few years back. A family ends up stranded for days in their car after taking a wrong turn in a blizzard. Cold and hungry, and after several hours into their ordeal, the father sets out to find help. He ultimately ends up freezing to death, but not before traveling in circles (which was evident by his tracks). This story made an impression on me because the family was found on an access road, a mere 1,500 feet off the highway.

Lighting strikes kill, on average, 100 people per year, and are especially dangerous for hikers on mountain peaks or ridges. To determine the distance of an approaching storm, count the seconds between thunder (the sound of lightening) and a flash. You can do this by counting slowly, "one-one thousand, two-one thousand." Five seconds is equivalent to one mile in distance, so if you count past seven seconds you're safe. However, if you count at or below five seconds, seek shelter.

Most backpacks have metal, so take it off and leave it several feet away. Find a dry surface, and crouch down on the balls of your feet. (This minimizes your surface area, decreasing your chances of being struck.) Don't huddle next to a single tree because it will act as a lightning rod; rather position yourself in the center of a cluster if possible. And although your natural instinct might be to take cover in a cave or depression—resist it. They are damp and wet, and the last place you should be in a thunderstorm.

I've already spent a fair amount of time covering bears, but because it merits repeating, I'll say it again. Bears don't like surprises, so if you're **hiking in bear country**, talk loudly, sing, or tie a bell to your backpack. Making yourself known is *especially* important if you're traveling a trail that has a lot of twists and turns. Also, if at all possible, walk with the wind at your back so the bears will smell you coming. But if they don't, and you happen upon one, do this:

1. Stay calm.
2. If he's unaware of you, back away quietly.
3. If he does spot you, identify yourself as a human by talking loudly, and make yourself as large as possible. (Again, by opening a jacket if you have one, or slowly waving your arms up and down).
4. Avoid eye contact.
5. If he runs away, slowly back away, then turn and go in the opposite direction, leaving the area.
6. If he doesn't retreat or approach, slowly back away and continue talking.
7. If he stands up, don't panic; this is a sign of curiosity, not aggression. He's just trying to get a better sniff or view of you.
8. If he approaches, stop, stand your ground, remain calm, and look for signs of aggression (teeth chomping, growling, head weaving, slapping the ground, or lip smacking).
9. If he charges, take out that bear spray you have harnessed at your waist because you listened to me, take aim, and fire. If you didn't listen to me and you don't have bear spray, fight back with everything you have.

Trail Finders

EveryTrail.com is an international hiking trail website, which pulls up trails matching your search criteria. I tested it out by going to *everytrail.com* and searched Lake Tahoe, CA. All of their featured trails have a picture next to the description, which includes rating, difficulty, length, and duration. Although several trails popped up, I'll use *Maggies Peaks* as an example.

This particular trail has a gorgeous view of Emerald Bay, gets five stars, and is a moderate three-mile hike which takes 1-3 hours to complete. It also has a brief description: *"Maggies Peaks overlook the rapturous blue waters of Emerald Bay, Lake Tahoe, Granite Lake and Desolation Wilderness."* Wow, sounds nice! And it only took me 30 seconds to find this trail. Then by clicking on *Maggies Peaks* you'll find even more details, more photos, maps, and trail tips.

AllTrails.com, a National Geographic subsidiary, is another excellent resource and works pretty much the same way. Although you have to spend a minute registering on their site, it's worth the effort (especially for dog owners) because this site lists dog-friendly trails. So, if you have any desire whatsoever to hit the trail during your camping trip, then check out these websites. Oh, and before I move on, you should know that there are apps for that! *Every Trail* and *All Trails* both offer free downloadable apps. So if you're a "fly by the seat of your pants" kind of gal (or you just run out of time before you set off), you may want to check them out.

All that said, if you're "old school" like me and you enjoy turning the pages of a book, then REI has a great selection of hiking books by destination. Or, you could hightail it down to your local bookstore, assuming your town still has one, that is.

Walking (aka Trekking) Poles

Until recently, I thought walking poles were silly. But here's the thing: they increase stamina by redistributing your pack's weight, minimize the impact on your knees and leg muscles, and make you more stable. Other benefits are improved circulation because your hands are in the desired "hands above the heart" position, and the rhythm created by walking with poles leads to a more relaxed, more regulated breathing. They're also great for moving stuff (e.g., spider webs, etc.), providing traction and balance and fighting off wild animals (God forbid). So if all of this makes sense to you, try renting a pair from *LowerGear.com* or better yet, purchase the poles I discussed in Chapter 3.

In Conclusion

Because I started this book stating the obvious about backpacking, I'm going to finish by reiterating *this* obvious. Don't attempt to hike Half Dome the first time you strap a daypack to your back. Spend some time easing into this activity because, like everything, it takes time to reach your stride. But once you do, and you hit the trail to wherever your Half Dome is, remember to take a moment to admire the view. And, once you get there, take a deep breath, blow it out, and think about how far you've come, figuratively *and* literally. Because, guess what? You're not *just* a Diva—you're a *camping* Diva!

CHAPTER 7 TIPS

- ✓ If at all possible, avoid hiking between 10 AM and 4 PM during the summer months (or
choose a heavily shaded trail).

- ✓ Wear new hiking boots around the house to break them in *before* you hit the trail. (Trust me, you'll thank me later.)

- ✓ Applying moleskin at the very first sign of a "hot spot" will help ward off blisters.

- ✓ Unless you have serious waterproofing on those hiking boots, you'll want to avoid getting them wet. Wet boots are the fastest ticket to Blisterville.

- ✓ Don't forget to take a trinket to exchange if you're planning to locate a geocache.

Epilogue

Tarzan and I have swung from many vines since that first camping trip to nowhere, and although the Diva in me resisted the role in the beginning, I have become, like it or not—Jane.

That being said, the fact that we're considering yet another upgrade makes me wonder. Is the Diva in me pushing out the Jane? If we go bigger, should we just stay home? That, my friends, is my dilemma. When is it time to let go of one vine and leap to another? I'm not sure, but I do know this: it IS a jungle out there. However, will I ever be happy camping in an asphalt one? I guess only time will tell…

RESOURCES

Camping 101
1. Backpacker.com: *What's in your Pack?*
2. YouTube.com/Appalachian Trail Conservancy: *Dispose of Waste Properly*
3. Wikipedia.org: *Leave No Trace*
4. Wikipedia.org: *Popup camper*
5. Wikipedia.org: *List of recreational vehicles*
6. CruiseAmerica.com (RV rentals)
7. El MonteRV.com (RV rentals)
8. AdventureinCamping.com (Mammoth RV set-up/rentals)
9. AckerRVRentals.com (Lake Tahoe RV set-up/rentals)
10. Glamping.com (reservation website)
11. GlampingHub.com (reservation website)
12. FaradayCage.org (lightening)

Campgrounds & Campsites
1. ReserveAmerica.com (reservation website)
2. Recreation.gov (reservation website)
3. AllStays.com (reservation website & app)
4. WeCampHere.com (reservation website & app)

Gear, (etc.)
1. REI.com/Learn/Expert Advice: *Layering Basics*
2. SierraTradingPost.com: *The Down vs Synthetic Guide*

3. REI.com/Learn/Expert Advice: *Rainwear: How to Choose*
4. Wikipedia.org: *Long underwear*
5. AnswerBag.com: *Which is warmer: thermal or silk underwear?*
6. Amazon.com (gear)
7. Campmor.com (gear)
8. REI.com (gear)
9. OutdoorGearLab.com (gear)
10. Wikipedia.org: *Bear-resistant food storage container*
11. ChicagoTribune.com: August 15, 2013/*Grizzly bear attacks, wounds two Yellowstone hikers* by Laura Zuckerman
12. HighCountryExplorations.com: *Emergency cell use/call devices*
13. Bushmarts.com (rope)
14. FeatherFriends.com (2-person sleeping bag)
15. CampSaver.com (sleeping bag for backpackers)
16. Tarptent.com (ultralight shelters)
17. Backpacker.com: *Is Iodine Effective?*
18. GeneratorRentals.com (self explanatory)
19. The Knot Guide (iOS app)
20. How to Tie Knots (Android app)
21. DuraCommLighting.com: *Why is LED Lighting Better?*
22. MosquitnoBand.com: *How-does-citronella-keep-bugs-away?*
23. Wikipedia.org*: DEET*
24. WebMD.com: *6 Insect Repellents Get High Marks*

Dining Outdoors

1. Spicesherpa.com: *6 Must-Have Spice Blends for Camping Cook Kits* (by Mark Bittman, 2010 Backpacker Magazine)
2. FoodNetwork.com: *50 Things to Grill in Foil*
3. DutchOvenDude.com (all inclusive Dutch oven cooking site)

Wild Things

1. NLM.NIH.gov/MedlinePlus: *Hantavirus*
2. CDC.gov: *Rabies/Other Wild Animals*
3. HumaneSociety.org: *Understanding Rabies*
4. RaccoonWorld.com: *Top 10 Raccoon Myths*
5. Wikipedia.org: *Fox*
6. WildSkunkRescue.com: *Skunks in Daylight–Shedding Light on a Dark Myth*
7. StinkyBusiness.org: *Skunks/Myths Versus Facts*
8. BearSmart.com/Becoming Bear Smart/Bear Smart in the Backcountry: *Securing Food, Garbage and Gear*
9. BearSmart.com/Becoming Bear Smart/Bear Smart in the Backcountry: *Bear Encounters/Play Safe in Bear Habitat*
10. BearSmart.com/Becoming Bear Smart/Bear Smart in the Backcountry: *Camping*
11. BearSmart.com/Resources/North America's Bears: *Dispelling Myths*
12. Wikipedia.org: *American Black Bear*
13. Defenders.org: *Basic Facts About Black Bears & Basic Facts About Grizzly Bears*

14. Wikipedia.org: *Grizzly Bear*

15. A-Z Animals.com: *Grizzly Bear*

16. Alaska.gov: *Kodiak Bear Fact Sheet*

17. DifferenceBetween.net: *Difference Between Black and Brown Bears*

18. StatisticBrain.com: *Bear Attack Statistics*

19. Wikipedia.org: *List of fatal bear attacks in North America*

20. DogBite.org: *2013 Dog bite fatalities*

21. Azgfd.gov: *Living With Mountain Lions*

22. Defenders.org: *Basic Facts About Mountain Lions*

23. MountainLion.org: *Frequently Asked Questions*

24. Wikipedia.org: *Bobcat*

25. Defenders.org: *Basic Facts About Bobcats*

26. PawNation.com/Animals: *Why Do Coyotes Howl in Packs?*

27. NationalGeographic.com/Animals/Mammal: *Coyote*

28. WikiHow.com: *Who to Act When Near a Coyote*

29. Defenders.org: *Basic Facts About Gray Wolves*

30. NewsWatch.NationalGeographic.com/2012/02/03/ *would-real-wolves-act-like-the-wolves-of-the-grey/*

31. Wikipedia.org: *Wolf Attacks on Humans*

32. ComingBackAlive.com/animalwolves: *Wolves & Coyotes*

33. WebMD.com/allergies/ss/*slideshow-bad-bugs:* (little critters)

34. Ask.com: *Where do bees live?*

35. About.com: *Do Bees Die After They Sting You?*

36. Orkin.com: *Stinging Pests*

37. Wikipedia.org: *Black widow spiders*

38. PoisonCenterTampa.org: *Stinging Caterpillars*

39. MedicineNet.com: *Chiggers*

40. Wikipedia.com: *Deer fly*

41. Wikipedia.com: *Fire ant*

42. CDC.gov/Plague: *Ecology and Transmission*

43. FleaBites.net: *Flea Bites on Humans–Pictures, Treatment & Prevention*

44. TheTopTens.com: *Top 10 Most Annoying Insects*

45. Ask.com: *Where do mosquitoes live?*

46. Wikipedia.org: *Mosquito*

47. ScropionWorlds.com (general information)

48. Slate.com: *How Deadly Are Scorpions?*

49. CDC.gov: *Venomous Snakes*

50. Nwf.org: *Rattlesnakes*

51. Copperhead-Snake.com (general information)

52. *CES.ncsu.edu: How Dangerous Are Copperhead Snakes?*

53. *CottonmouthSnake.org (general information)*

54. PawNation.com/Animals: *Where Do Cottonmouths Live?*

55. Wikipedia.org: *Coral snake*

56. WikiHow.com: *How to Tell the Difference Between a King Snake and a Coral Snake*

57. NLM.nih.gov/medlineplus (National Library of Medicine, National Institutes of Health): *Snake Bites*

58. CDC.gov: *Ticks*

59. Poison-Ivy.org: *Poison ivy, oak, & sumac*

60. MedicineNet.com: *Outsmarting Poison Ivy and It's Cousins*

61. TecLabsInc.com: *Beware of Burning Poison ivy & Oak*

With Children & Dogs

1. Blog.KOA.com/ *10-Best-Apps-For-Camping-and-Outdoors*
2. Coleman.com/downloads (Coleman's Creepy Campfire Tales app)
3. MyNatureApps.com (My Nature Animal Tracks*)*
4. VitoTechnology.com (Star Walk app)
5. ProjectNoah.org/mobile (iOS & Android app)
6. WRVO.org: *How the sun and your car can create a dangerous situation*
7. SteveDalePetWorld.com *Dogs Die in Hot Cars*
8. GGWeather.com/heat: *Heatstroke Deaths of Children in Vehicles* by Jan Null, CCM Department of Meteorology & Climate Science, San Jose State University
9. Patheos.com: *5 reasons to obey the lease law (yes, I'm talking to you)*
10. Nolo.com: Leash Laws
11. OPishPosh.com: *Top 10 Most Dangerous Dog Breeds to be Wary Of*

Hiking

1. EveryTrail.com (online trail finder)
2. AllTrails.com (online trail finder w/ pet friendly trails)
3. SectionHiker.com: *Day Hikers' Ten Essential Guide*
4. HikingDude.com: *Water for Hiking*
5. OutdoorGearLab.com: *Ten Reasons for Trekking Poles*
6. Geocaching.com (online source/GPS treasure hunts)
7. WikiHow.com: *How to Go Geocaching*

8. GrizzlyDiscoveryCtr.com/Education: *Camping & Hiking in Bear Country*
9. HikeSafe.com (safety and general information)
10. NPS.gov (National Park Service): *Hiking Safety*

ADDITIONAL READING

Camping 101

1. REI.com/Learn/Expert Advice: *Backpacking for Beginners*
2. REI.*com*/Learn/Expert Advice: *Hygiene and Sanitation in the Backcountry*
3. AllMountainSports.com: *Hygiene and Femininity in the Backcountry*
4. REI.com/Learn/Expert Advice: *Campsite Comfort and Organization*
5. YouTube.com: *How to Hook Up a Trailer Properly* (various videos)
6. RV-Roadtrips.TheFunTimesGuide.com (all inclusive website)
7. REI.com/Learn/Expert Advice: *Campfire Basics*
8. National Wildlife Federation: *Campfire Safety*

Campgrounds & Campsites

1. Sunset.com/travel/outdoor-adventure/find-your-perfect-campground:
   - *Perfect campgrounds for first-timers*
   - *Perfect campgrounds for families*
   - *Perfect campgrounds for amenities junkies*
   - *Perfect campgrounds for secret spot hunters*

- *Perfect campgrounds for comfort cravers*
- *Perfect campgrounds for adventurers*
- *Perfect campgrounds for solitude seekers*

2. Backpacker.com/october_2007_destinations_ americas_best_campsites/destinations/11035: *America's Best Campsites*
3. Greatist.com/fitness/best-camping-united-states: *The 26 Best Places to Pitch a Tent in the U.S.*
4. TripleBlaze.com: *The Best Campgrounds in the United States*
5. *Northern California Camping, A Complete Guide to Tent & RV Camping* by Tom Stienstra (highlights specific campgrounds, etc.)

Gear, (etc.)

1. Backpacker.com: *Ask A Bear: Electric Fence As a Deterrent?*
2. REI.com/Learn/Expert Advice: *GPS Receivers: How to Choose*
3. REI.com/Learn/Expert Advice: *Socks for Hiking: How to Choose*
4. REI.com/Learn/Expert Advice: *Solar Chargers & Portable Power*
5. REI.com/Learn/Expert Advice: *Sun Protection Clothing Basics*
6. REI.com/Learn/Expert Advice: *Tent for camping: How to Choose*

Dining Outdoors
1. REI/com/Learn/Expert Advice: *Meal Planning for Backpackers*
2. LoveTheOutdoors.com: *Camp Cooking Tips*
3. Culinaryarts.about.com: *Cooking at High Altitude* by Danilo Alfaro

Wild Things
1. OutsideOnline.com: *Shoot or Spray? The Best Way to Stop a Charging Bear by Nick Heil*
2. Los Angeles Times: September 7, 2014: *Mountain lion attacks 6-year-old boy in Silicon Valley,* by Teresa Watanabe
3. UABMedicine.org: *What's the best way to remove a bee stinger?*
4. KnowledgeWeighsNothing.com: *"U.S. Venomous Spiders, State by State"*
5. MayoClinic.org: *First Aid*

With Children & Dogs
1. REI.com/Learn/Expert Advice: *Backpacking With Kids*
2. REI.com/Learn/Expert Advice: *Kids & Camping*
3. REI.com/Learn/Expert Advice: *Hiking or Backpacking With Your Dog*

Hiking
1. REI.com/Learn/Expert Advice: *Breaking in Your Hiking Boots*
2. REI.com/Learn/Expert Advice: *Hydration Basics*
3. REI.com/Learn/Expert Advice: *Lost in the Backcountry? How to React*

INDEX

NOTES

www.ingramcontent.com/pod-product-compliance
Lightning Source LLC
Chambersburg PA
CBHW070108290526
45789CB00005B/1969